SBA Loans

Lew Gaiter, Jr., J.D. and Roberta E. Lonsdale

Made E-Z

NOTICE:

THIS PRODUCT IS NOT INTENDED TO PROVIDE LEGAL ADVICE. IT CONTAINS GENERAL INFORMATION FOR EDUCATIONAL PURPOSES ONLY. PLEASE CONSULT AN ATTORNEY IN ALL LEGAL MATTERS. THIS PRODUCT WAS NOT NECESSARILY PREPARED BY A PERSON LICENSED TO PRACTICE LAW IN YOUR STATE.

SBA Loans Made E-Z™
© Copyright 2001 Made E-Z Products, Inc.
Printed in the United States of America

MADE E-Z
PRODUCTS

384 South Military Trail
Deerfield Beach, FL 33442
Tel. 954-480-8933
Fax 954-480-8906

http://www.MadeE-Z.com
All rights reserved.

3 4 5 6 7 8 9 10

SBA Loans Made E-Z™
Lew Gaiter, Jr., J.D. and Roberta Lonsdale

Important Notice

Table of contents

How to use this guide

E-Z Legal's Made E-Z™ Guides can help you achieve an important legal objective conveniently, efficiently and economically. But it is important to properly use this guide if you are to avoid later difficulties.

◆ Carefully read all information, warnings and disclaimers concerning the legal forms in this guide. If after thorough examination you decide that you have circumstances that are not covered by the forms in this guide, or you do not feel confident about preparing your own documents, consult an attorney.

◆ Complete each blank on each legal form. Do not skip over inapplicable blanks or lines intended to be completed. If the blank is inapplicable, mark "N/A" or "None" or use a dash. This shows you have not overlooked the item.

◆ Always use pen or type on legal documents—never use pencil.

◆ Avoid erasures and "cross-outs" on final documents. Use photocopies of each document as worksheets, or as final copies. All documents submitted to the court must be printed on one side only.

◆ Correspondence forms may be reproduced on your own letterhead if you prefer.

◆ Whenever legal documents are to be executed by a partnership or corporation, the signatory should designate his or her title.

◆ It is important to remember that on legal contracts or agreements between parties all terms and conditions must be clearly stated. Provisions may not be enforceable unless in writing. All parties to the agreement should receive a copy.

◆ Instructions contained in this guide are for your benefit and protection, so follow them closely.

◆ You will find a glossary of useful terms at the end of this guide. Refer to this glossary if you encounter unfamiliar terms.

◆ Always keep legal documents in a safe place and in a location known to your spouse, family, personal representative or attorney.

About the authors

Lew Gaiter, Jr., J.D., president and owner of ZachAar Consultants, Inc., financial consultants for small businesses, is a graduate of the University of Denver School of Law. He is also one of the founders and former president of the first minority-operated commercial bank established in the State of Colorado. Lew successfully owned and managed a variety of businesses over the past 30 years. His areas of expertise include solving businesses' cash-flow problems, and purchasing and expanding existing businesses.

ZachAar Consultants has been involved in local real estate investments consistent with Denver's growth into the 21st Century and expanded its consulting services outside of the Metropolitan Denver area and Colorado.

Roberta E. Lonsdale, a technical writing consultant providing services to a variety of clients, holds a Certificate of Advanced Studies in Technical Writing from the University of Denver and B.S. and M.S. degrees in geology. During her career, she published more than 15 technical papers and abstracts as well as the novel, *Colorado Gold*. Roberta teaches technical writing, editing and industrial communications at the Metropolitan State College of Denver.

Roberta specializes in preparing written and oral communications in support of corporate or administrative objectives, using more than 25 years of applied communications, business, and technical experience. She is experienced with small, minority, and woman-owned businesses.

Lew and Roberta are co-authors of *The Entrepreneur's Handbook*, published by SterlingHouse Publishers.

About the SBA loan programs

1

Chapter 1

About the SBA loan programs

The last two decades have proved that small businesses, including mom-and-pop sized operations, were the leaders in bringing about technological advances in industry and business; they also provide a significant source of employment for the country. When the Small Business Administration (SBA) was created, the government demonstrated its awareness that small- and medium-sized businesses represent the backbone of business and industry in this country. Through its assistance, the Small Business Administration helps businesses in this country to thrive, grow, and prosper.

The Small Business Administration is a significant resource for women- and minority-owned and disadvantaged businesses desiring to enter the business mainstream. By assisting these businesses, the government supports a stronger and more diverse economy.

The U.S. Small Business Administration was established by statute in 1953 for the purpose of assisting small- and medium-sized businesses to procure, grow, and become successful. The Small Business Administration seeks to achieve its goals by assisting these businesses in areas where they can't achieve financial and other support through normal business channels without experiencing unreasonable requirements.

DEFINITION

The Small Business Act defines a *small business* based on size standards defined in dollars, and by the type of business identified by Standard Industrial Codes. Small businesses are defined by Brock and Evans (1986) as those with fewer than 500 employees (for the employment and value added measures) or those with sales of under $5 million in 1958 dollars (for the sales measure). Although this book was published more than a decade ago, Brock and Evans provide good information relevant to the growth and development of small businesses, their importance in this country's economy and in technical advances.

Standard Industrial Classification codes, a federal standard numbering system used to identify a company's function by industry, is also used by the Small Business Administration in defining a small business. You'll be asked to determine which of the codes applies to your business and to enter those codes on certain forms. The codes are published by the U.S. Bureau of the Budget and the manual is available from the Government Printing Office, Small Business Administration, and through the Internet.

SBA loan programs

The Small Business Administration, governmental agencies, and non-profit organizations that provide financial and other assistance to small businesses established criteria that borrowers must meet to receive assistance. The Small Business Administration has various loan and technical assistance programs for eligible small businesses, and for community organizations that support small businesses.

Although the Small Business Administration doesn't issue funds directly, they do guarantee a percentage of a loan made by commercial lenders and other organized institutions. This guarantee provides greater incentive to the lenders by diminishing the risk factor in the loans. These loans are usually issued for the purchase of real estate for business use, construction, leasehold improvements, purchase of furniture and fixtures, machinery and equipment, inventory, and working capital.

note Commercial banks represent lenders who work most closely with the Small Business Administration.

Although other programs exist and are defined in the glossary of this guide, the major loan programs used by borrowers are:

- **7(a) Guaranteed Loan Program**

    The 7(a) Guaranteed Loan Program is the most popular and is funded through private-sector commercial lenders, commercial banks, and non-profit organizations. This program helps to ensure that reasonable funds are available and affordable to small firms located in areas having either high unemployment or large numbers of low-income residents.

- **Low Documentation Loan Program**

    The LowDoc Loan Program refers to the low number of documents required between the lender and the Small Business Administration. The information you provide the lender is not reduced—but, the information provided to the Small Business Administration is, and your information remains in the lender's care for the benefit of the Small Business Administration. For the borrower, the most important part of the program is probably the fast turnaround on loan approval. Everything else being equal, the approval for a LowDoc loan is weighted more heavily towards character and credit rather than collateral.

- **Certified Development Company (504 Loan) Program**

  This program is popular for purchasing land, machinery and equipment, and remodeling the business' real property. These loans are available on a long-term basis of 25 years or more for amortization. The lender, the borrower, and a certified 504 development company provide the funds for the loan and the Small Business Administration guarantees the loan.

Small Business Administration loan programs are listed in the Appendix in Table 1.1, and Specialized Small Business Administration programs are shown in Table 1.2. Other government loans available to small businesses are listed in Table 1.3, although others may be available.

Community Programs

The community programs supported by the Small Business Administration are usually non-profit or other organizations that provide business education and assistance. These loans are smaller, but are guaranteed in some percentage by the Small Business Administration. Many of these programs are operated by your state through Small Business Development Centers and by organizations targeting special groups such as minorities, women, and disadvantaged business owners.

SBA technical assistance programs

For either small business owners or entrepreneurs planning to start-up a business, the Small Business Administration offers several programs to assist you. Two popular programs are the Business Information Centers (BICs) and the Service Corps of Retired Executives (SCORE).

One of the best technical assistance resources offered by the Small Business Administration is the Business Information Center, described in the

Appendix. These centers are staffed by a full-time SBA manager and assisted by SCORE volunteers. The centers are sponsored by local businesses and typically have one or more of the following resources:

- publication library

- video/audio library

- computer facilities

- SCORE counseling

- SCORE workshops

- SCORE business information directory

SCORE is probably the best known technical and management group sponsored by the Small Business Administration. The group consists of more than 12,000 volunteers who are retired successful business executives and owners. The program matches business-management counselors with present and prospective small business owners and entrepreneurs. To apply for this program, use SBA Standard Form 641—Request for Counseling, discussed in Chapter 6 (*Preparing other SBA forms*).

Roadmap of this guide

Although you may be a successful small business entrepreneur knowledgeable about your products or services, you may not be skilled in the procedures for obtaining financial and other assistance from organizations such as the Small Business Administration, commercial lenders, or other associations. This guide is designed to help you to understand the small business loan application process and to effectively use the necessary forms.

Many small business owners and entrepreneurs have sought the assistance of consultants, although they could have completed the forms themselves. This guide contains the required and optional forms and a thorough explanation on how to interpret and prepare each form. Interpretation of the forms and their associated instructions can be a challenge and the legalese may be difficult to understand, even with repeated readings.

 This guide is not intended to help you determine how much, when, and what assistance you need in a business start-up. Another book by the same authors, *The Entrepreneur's Handbook—How to Start, Operate, and Run Your Own Business,* covers this area and is available through SterlingHouse Publishers, Pittsburgh, Pennsylvania.

The seven chapters of this guide cover information for preparing your loan proposal package. Depending upon your personal knowledge, background and experience, you may choose to first read the chapters that are of greatest interest to you. If you are less familiar with this type of material, you may find that reading the chapters in sequence will be the most instructive. You don't have to read or use the chapters in the order in which they are presented.

Chapters 2 through 7 address the preparation of a Small Business Administration loan proposal package. Chapter 2 (Developing Your Loan Proposal Package) presents information on loan package elements, a suggested approach and guidance about preparing owner and organization descriptions. Chapter 3 (Describing History, Operations, and Marketing), presents guidance about preparing loan package elements relevant to the business. Understanding financial matters (Chapter 4) contains information about the financial portions of your loan proposal package.

Chapters 5 and 6 present information and guidance about preparing Small Business Administration forms. In Chapter 5 (Preparing Required SBA Forms), you'll learn how to complete an array of complex and duplicative government forms that may confuse the uninitiated. In addition to required forms, Chapter 6 (Preparing Other SBA Forms) contains guidance relevant to other Small Business Administration forms that may be useful to you and your proposed business.

Chapter 7 (Compiling Your Loan Proposal Package) shows you a method for finalizing your loan package and presenting the package in a professional manner.

Tables and figures referred to within the text can be found in the Appendices in the back of the book. The Forms section of this guide contains copies of the forms and thorough instructions for completing each one. You will also find a Glossary containing commonly used business words included for your convenience, as well as selected U.S. Small Business Administration and other resources for entrepreneurs in the Resources section of this guide.

Developing your loan proposal package

2

Chapter 2

Developing your loan proposal package

What you'll find in this chapter:

➠ Why you need a business plan

➠ Compiling the loan proposal package

➠ Essential additions to your package

➠ Ways to indicate your business competency

➠ Building an organizational chart

Many small businesses fail because the owner has not taken the time to develop a proper business plan. In recognition of this fact, the Small Business Administration requires a business plan as part of your loan application (see the Appendix for other Small Business Administration resources). However, if you develop a loan proposal package as outlined here and in the following chapters, the package will also suffice as your business plan.

With a few exceptions, the organization of this and subsequent chapters is generally consistent with the order you'll use when you're finally ready to compile your loan proposal package for presentation. Guidance on compiling the loan package for presentation, after the elements are prepared, is presented in Chapter 7 (Compiling Your Loan Proposal Package). Loan package elements; tax, legal, and other information; and owner and organization descriptions are discussed in this chapter.

Loan package elements

Generally speaking, loan package elements are presented in a narrative format, although tables and charts may enhance some information. Small Business Administration information is presented about standardized forms.

Order of Presentation

Lenders don't usually provide you with information on loan package content unless they have their own form. However, because you aren't a professional loan packager, the lender will be glad to tell you what information is expected—but not necessarily how to present the material. Don't be afraid to ask.

 note One of your jobs is to present the information in a logical manner that is easy for the lender to find and use.

The objective of preparing a loan proposal package is to present yourself and your ideas to a potential lender in the most constructive and favorable light. The lender wants to feel comfortable that the borrowed funds are in good hands and will look for the elements shown in Table 2.1. Loan packages should always contain these elements. This table, provided for your convenience, represents the general outline of your loan proposal. Depending upon your situation, elements may be added or removed.

CAUTION If the lender requires specific information, be sure that you understand exactly what the lender is requesting. Otherwise, the individual reviewing the package may have difficulty locating the requested material and this could delay your application or result in rejection.

Suggested Approach

Preparing a loan proposal package isn't an overwhelming task if you accomplish the work one chunk at a time. Keep in mind that:

- If you take the time to gather your information first, the process is easier.

- Your order of preparation need not be the same as the order of presentation.

- You don't have to start at the beginning.

- Do the easiest tasks first.

> If the descriptive portions are easier, start a draft of these elements—if the numbers are easier, begin with the financial information.

No matter where you choose to begin, the first step is to compile, sort, and organize relevant materials. Establish a filing system that works for you. A convenient way to compile your materials is to either prepare a three-ring binder with index dividers or establish manila folders for each section, or use a combination of binder and folders.

If you decide to use a binder and don't want to punch holes in your original documents, either photocopy them or use inexpensive top-loading sheet protectors that are guaranteed not to lift the print off your documents. Insert the documents you have on hand and use colored paper to identify those documents you need, but either have not yet located, acquired, or prepared.

> Using colored paper with the name of the missing document written on the top gives you a quick way of visually determining your progress.

If you're unsure where to begin, the loan package elements shown in Table 2.2 are grouped so that similar items can be prepared together for greater efficiency. Either choose one of these groups to begin your work or follow the suggested order of preparation. Refer to the listed chapters for a discussion of each element and guidance on content.

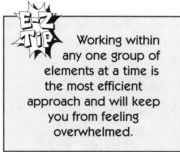

Working within any one group of elements at a time is the most efficient approach and will keep you from feeling overwhelmed.

You may find that completing the Small Business Administration forms first will give you more insight into your total proposal and may be an excellent starting point. Or, you could start the loan proposal by developing your own resume and that of other key personnel who will be involved in your business as either an owner or manager. This helps you: (1) focus on relevant skills and backgrounds; and (2) plan how to present work and personal histories to your advantage.

Use the information from the resumes and interviews with the other owners or managers to develop a narrative profile describing each individual. Next, use your ideas to design an organization chart showing the duties and operations within the proposed organization.

note You can find ideas for organization charts from library books and/or use commercially available software.

Tax, legal, and other information

Depending upon the type of business you're proposing and your personal history, the volume of relevant tax, legal, and other information will vary. This tax and legal information is presented at the end of a loan proposal package, but it's discussed now so you may refer to the material as you develop your loan proposal package.

Tax Information

If you were born on this planet and reached adulthood, you probably have tax records. The loan proposal package must include your personal Internal Revenue Service (IRS) returns filed for the previous three tax years. In some cases, you may be asked to provide additional information about your tax returns. Be prepared.

Both your personal and business tax returns (if applicable) give the lender an idea of how much money are used to handling.

Legal Information

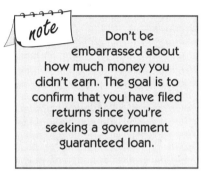

The type of legal information you'll need to compile depends upon the proposed business. Typical legal information is shown in Table 2.3. Collect this information and store it either in your binder or in your manila folders.

note Don't be embarrassed about how much money you didn't earn. The goal is to confirm that you have filed returns since you're seeking a government guaranteed loan.

Other Supporting Information

If you have additional information that supports your loan application, compile the documents and store them in your binder or manila folders for later use. Table 2.4 lists the type of supporting information that may be useful in your loan proposal package.

If you don't have this type of supporting information on hand, and think it may be useful to you, identify those elements that are most supportive and obtain the documents as you're preparing your loan package. For example, it isn't too late to ask for letters of reference from business or personal contacts.

Owner and organization descriptions

In this section, you have the opportunity to demonstrate that you and your proposed management team are fully competent-by virtue of acquired

> **note** A loan proposal package is also a marketing document. The lender must feel comfortable that the proposed owner or owners are competent to successfully run the business.

skills or cumulative experience-to achieve business goals, generate a positive cash flow, and meet financial obligations (i.e., pay back the loan on time).

You have the opportunity to demonstrate your competence through preparation of resumes, owner and manager profiles, and organization charts. The material you provide for these elements must be relevant to the proposed business. If you're like most individuals beginning a new business, your background is probably related to the type of business that you're about to enter. If it's not, it should be—remember, a retired rocket scientist probably would not make a good dairy farmer.

Mr. Harvey Mackay is an author and business executive with Mackay Envelope Corporation of Minneapolis, Minnesota, who writes a syndicated newspaper column. In the December 21, 1997, edition of The Denver Post, Mr. Mackay discusses the heart bypass surgery of Boris Yeltsin, president of Russia. The point he makes in this article regards the experience factor.

> **E-Z TIP** An impressive resume isn't what interests the lender. The lender is interested in your background and knowledge you have of the business. He must determine if you have what it takes to make the business work.

Mr. Yeltsin chose to have his surgery performed by an American surgeon rather than one of the many fine heart surgeons in Russia. Evidently, Russian surgeons tend to operate on the elite and therefore, don't have the same broad base of experience as do American surgeons (who don't ask their patients for credentials before operating). Therefore, American surgeons have experienced many more procedures than their Russian counterparts.

Sometimes it is practical and desirable to employ family members in the start-up of a new business and may, in fact, hold tax advantages for you and your family member. However, what the lender will be looking for in your loan proposal package is your assurance that the individual family member you have selected for a particular position and assigned responsibilities is capable. If you can't prove that the family member is capable on paper, then

the individual may not have the skills you need. This represents increased risk for the lender and for you as the owner (think about how awkward it would be to fire an aunt, uncle, cousin, brother, or sister...not to mention your parents, spouse, or children).

note Make sure that the content of your resume is supportive of your loan application. If your resume reflects that you have chosen a business in which you have no experience or expertise, the number of willing lenders will dwindle rapidly to zero.

Resumes

The purpose of including a resume in a loan proposal package is to provide the lender with a quick overview of your experience, skill, education, and accomplishments as they support of your loan application. If you're a sole proprietor, a resume for yourself will suffice. If your business is a partnership or corporation, then you must include a resume for each owner and all key managers.

note Your resume is important because it may be the lender's first introduction to you, an aspiring entrepreneur.

You want the lender to discover quickly that you have the basic skills and experience necessary to succeed in your chosen venture. Here's your chance to gather together the pertinent information for presentation on one page, two at the most.

You'll find a number of excellent books on how to write a resume in any library or bookstore. The key to writing a resume is to remember that you're preparing a summary—the word is derived from the French term *resumer* meaning "to summarize."

If you already have a suitable resume, you may not need to prepare one. Or, you may wish to re-work your old resume to be more supportive of your loan application. However, it isn't unusual to re-work resumes for other purposes. If you need to prepare one, follow the steps listed in Table 2.5.

> **E-Z TIP** If writing your own resume is difficult, look for an individual or writing service specializing in resume preparation. Even if you choose to have a professional prepare your resume, you'll need to gather the applicable information described in Table 2.5, Step No. 1.

Once the resumes are ready, you now have material to develop a narrative description of the owner and manager profiles. At this time you should consider sketching out an organization chart, as discussed below.

You don't have to be a genius with a fabulous background and a broad skill base to demonstrate your qualifications. However, you'll want to assure the lender that you have a background appropriate for the proposed venture. To do this, you'll need to present yourself in the most favorable light–make yourself look good without stretching the facts (this would be unethical).

In order to show the ability of the owner and managers to successfully operate the company and manage its finances, you must include information relating to each individual's personal and business history of successes and failures.

> **note** You shouldn't be ashamed of presenting failures as well as your successes. Both count as experience and both represent aspects that brought you to your present position.

The more experience you have, the better your understanding will be.

For example, Mr. Butler wants to start a mobile oil change and lubrication business, although he never before owned or operated a business. Mr. Butler has more than 10 years of work experience in the plumbing industry as an apprentice, journeyman, and finally a master plumber. His only relevant experience was formal training in high school automobile mechanics. This experience was presented three times on his resume–under qualifications and experience; certifications, training, and memberships; and education–each time with a slightly different twist (Figure 2.1).

In addition to his auto mechanics skills, Mr. Butler had some management and scheduling experience as a union member. He was able to demonstrate his negotiating skills as a liaison between union members and management. Although these experiences aren't directly related to the mobile oil and lube industry, they are skills pertinent to successfully managing a business, and therefore supportive of his loan application.

Owner and manager profiles

The key to developing a winning narrative is to demonstrate competence. Look through your resume, identify those aspects that you want to expand, and ask yourself how you can most favorably present them.

Because you're proposing a start-up business, you most likely don't have an experienced management team. In some instances a group of people may form an organization and a team for the purpose of starting a new business. These individuals are probably experienced professionals and have already met with some success within the industry they are about to enter. However, for a business start-up, this situation is more the exception than the rule.

The purpose of this section is to identify and present the owner and manager, and their respective job titles and responsibilities. Spend some time thinking about the owner and manager profiles. You'll want the descriptions to be fully supportive by demonstrating how each individual's background contributes to the proposed business.

In Mr. Butler's case, the emphasis was placed on his earlier formal training in high school automobile mechanics and his experience in scheduling and negotiations gained through his subsequent work experience. Excerpts from his owner and manager profile are shown in Figure 2.2 and give an example of how to present relevant experience in the most favorable light.

Not every owner and manager will have a comprehensive background in every aspect of owning and managing a business. If you have a weak area, identify the area and propose a solution.

Depending upon the type of proposed business and the number of intended employees, add brief paragraphs for each key employee demonstrating their competence and relevance to their assigned roles. An example for a public relations firm art director is shown in Figure 2.3.

Organization Chart

DEFINITION

Engineers use flow charts in design work to demonstrate process steps and interactions. An *organization chart* is a modified flow chart used for business purposes to demonstrate the relationships and interactions between positions, individuals, and areas of operation.

Organization charts are powerful visual tools for illustrating your company's organization and lines of authority. Use the organization chart to show each position and who will fill it; and how many employees you're planning to have during the first year of operation.

Conventional organization charts show the lines of authority generally flowing from the top down with the owner, manager, or board of directors shown at the top and positions with decreasing authority shown sequentially below. Each position and individual filling the position is shown in a box with lines connecting the boxes. Here is a typical organization box indicating the position and name of the individual filling the position:

> **Chief Executive Officer**
> **Ms. Jane Doe**

Most companies operate efficiently using a clearly defined top-down, line-of-authority organizational structure.

An example of a simple flow chart with a conventional organization is shown in Figure 2.4.

DEFINITION Some businesses, however, work better when the organization is more flexible. For these companies, a matrix or modified-matrix management approach may be more suitable. *Matrix management* differs from the conventional approach in that the manager draws from a pool of qualified individuals to form a team that's best suited to meet project needs.

Figure 2.5 shows the modified matrix management organization for a public relations firm. For this company, the ability of managers to identify teams allows the best fit between client project needs and available personnel.

note The conventional organization chart has the advantage of identifying duties and responsibilities so that each employee knows what is expected at each level.

Notice that the account managers are shown on one line and that the boxes are interconnected, indicating shared responsibilities. The same is true for the second line of creative services personnel. The managers of this organization have the freedom to build the most suitable teams and assign managers to the benefit of their clients.

If you have trouble designing an organization chart, there are various software programs available to help you in developing one appropriate for your business.

Describing your business plan

3

Chapter 3

Describing your business plan

Three important elements in developing your loan proposal package are:

1) Descriptions of the history, or evolution of your ideas to start a business

2) Proposed business operations

3) Marketing

Written narratives demonstrate to the lender that you studied each element and developed plans that help to ensure the success of your proposed business.

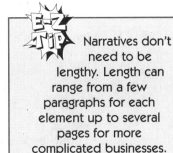

E-Z TIP Narratives don't need to be lengthy. Length can range from a few paragraphs for each element up to several pages for more complicated businesses.

By preparing these written narratives, you demonstrate to the lender that you progressed systematically with your idea, and fully thought through your business approach.

The lender has other proposals to review in addition to yours—if you want it read, keep it brief. Clear and concise narratives act to your advantage and assist the lender in the review process.

> **E-Z TIP**
> Say things one time and in one place. Imagine the confusion that results if you mention your ownership percentage using three different places and numbers because you changed the percentage as your project evolved and didn't correct each entry!

History

Because we are discussing new and start-up businesses there is, of course, no company or business history. Therefore, your personal history that brought about your desire to start a business can be inserted into this part. The purpose of the history is to describe how you made the decision to start the proposed business, the trials and tribulations you experienced, and the present status and anticipated future of the proposed business.

The history should contain information about:

- your concept

- when you developed the concept and its subsequent evolution

- your personal background and how it suits the proposed business

- your potential partners and/or key personnel

- good and bad experiences in running and growing the business

- present status of the business

- future outlook for the business

Several examples are presented here to give you an idea about content and the presentation mode for describing the business start-up history. Assume that you're a skilled brain surgeon and just retired from a major area hospital after 20 years of service. As a second career, you decided to begin a home health-care business to service individuals disabled by brain injury. You discussed this proposal with your spouse, who has 20 years of experience as a corporate business manager, and your daughter, who is a trained nurse with two years of experience. Your assets are adequate to support your loan application. You named your proposed business "Personal Home Health Care." A sample history is shown in Figure 3.1.

If you aren't a brain surgeon, assume that you were a cashier and waitperson in the restaurant business for 10 years. You have an associate degree in business administration from the local community college and your spouse is a skilled and experienced chef. The two of you believe that the number of affordable family-style restaurants in your growing community are too few to meet the demand. You own your home and have a modest savings account adequate to support your loan application. You want to call your restaurant, "Home Cookin' Diner." A sample history is shown in Figure 3.2.

Although these two scenarios are different, each contains elements for success. The challenge is to present these ideas in a way that demonstrates your ability to own and operate a successful business.

Business description (operation)

The business description section contains proposed business operations, procedures, and work-flow projections. Use this section to focus on how the business will operate and refer to the description shown in Table 3.1.

Read through the list of questions presented in the first column of Table 3.1 before reading the examples so that you have an understanding of the scope before you see how each has been addressed. Examples vary among manufacturing, retail, and service businesses. The type of business described in the example is indicated in the first column in parentheses. Answer these questions for yourself before beginning to develop a narrative.

> **E-Z TIP**
> Address the questions that are easiest for you first and save the most difficult ones for last. Keep in mind that you may not have to answer every question.

Once you have answered the questions applicable to your proposed business, you are ready to string the answers together to form a draft of your narrative. The structure of the narrative doesn't have to follow the order shown in Table 3.1 and should be presented in the order most supportive of your loan proposal package or most logical for your business type. However, if you're unsure of the order of presentation, follow that shown in Table 3.1.

> **E-Z TIP**
> After stringing your answers together, smooth the narrative by adding transition sentences and paragraphs so that the text flows evenly for the convenience of the lender.

Your draft might read something like the example presented in Figure 3.3 for a service business (see the Appendices).

Marketing

In its simplest form, marketing means "to sell" and includes product origination and design, development, distribution, advertising, promotion, publicity, and market analysis, but not necessarily in that order. You can prepare the marketing plan yourself, although in some cases, depending on your funds, you may find it practical to either hire a marketing consultant or enroll in a marketing seminar to help you develop your marketing plan.

Just as with resumes, there are many marketing books available, ranging from classic and conventional tomes to more colorful books like *Guerrilla Marketing Weapons* by Jay Conrad Levinson (1990). Your marketing strategy, however, will partially be driven by the type of proposed business you launch.

The marketing approach for a retail business, for example, will differ considerably from that for a manufacturing business because the "audience" is different.

Lenders look for and expect to find statements concerning a number of issues relating to marketing of your chosen product or service, such as:

- target audience

- demographics

- market share

- competition

- pricing structure

- advertising

- plans for the future

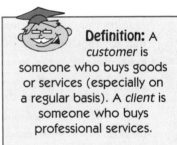

Definition: A *customer* is someone who buys goods or services (especially on a regular basis). A *client* is someone who buys professional services.

Addressing these elements clearly calls for homework on your part. The lender wants to see that you have thought through each element and have a plan for proceeding. Reference and research materials abound. Your local library is an excellent resource for finding statistics to support your marketing plan. State and federal offices publish information on demographics. Existing businesses of a similar nature are another source of information. Some companies, such as Dunn & Bradstreet, have call-in services for finding the number of similar businesses existing within a certain radius of your proposed location. An Internet search may provide additional information or sources, such as on-line access to trade groups. Use these resources to support your marketing plan.

> *note*
> Direct-mail marketing is an effective form of advertising. If you receive a three-percent response, your campaign was a success! If you offer something free, response may be as a high as 10 percent.

In developing your marketing plan, you can use the same approach taken in developing the narrative of your business operations description. Read the questions listed in the first column of Table 3.2 to gain a sense of scope before reading the examples in the second column. The examples vary for different types of businesses.

It's not what you want to sell that counts, it's what people want to buy that counts. Choosing a product or service that people want to buy makes an enormous difference in your sales potential.

As before, answer the questions for your proposed business and string your answers together to form a draft of the narrative. Not every question may be relevant to your proposed type of business. Also, start with the easiest question first and use the information you developed from your research.

Smooth your narrative with transition sentences and paragraphs. A sample marketing plan for a mobile lube business is shown in Figure 3.4

Presenting your financial summary

4

Chapter 4

Presenting your financial summary

A financial summary of your company can be used either to assess your financial position for a specific purpose, such as month-to-month or year-to-year comparisons; or as part of a loan proposal package. This discussion focuses on the use of the financial summary for presenting information as part of either a Small Business Administration or conventional commercial loan application and assumes that you already have some basic grasp of the material.

Your summary should include short paragraphs for each part of the loan package financial presentation and should contain supporting information regarding the ability of the owner and managers to:

- successfully operate the company and manage its finances

- implement internal cash controls

- explain responsibilities of owners and managers

- assign employment and positions to family members

- prepare present and past financial histories of your company

Certain elements listed here are relevant to preparing a financial summary, but aren't discussed in this section. Instead, please refer to the information presented in Chapter 2 (Developing Your Loan Proposal Package).

Because this guide examines the strategy for preparing a loan proposal package for a new business, our discussion is limited to those aspects relevant to a start-up business.

Internal cash controls

An important financial matter is the ability of the owner and manager to implement effective internal cash controls. In one form or another, cash is an important business asset. For this reason, it's necessary for the owner and manager to control the flow of cash through the business so that the cash benefits the business operation.

The lender will want assurance that you have assigned responsibilities to individuals who have the background and capability to handle the designated responsibilities.

DEFINITION

Internal cash controls differ from cash flow. *Internal cash controls* have to do with what happens to the funds collected from sales and how the collected cash flows through your business on its way to the bank. Cash flow is a determinant of whether or not you have enough cash moving through your business to cover your operational costs.

Internal cash controls are usually of more concern in businesses that aren't asset based, such as a service business that typically has no assets that are convertible to cash. Instead, the income is based on providing a specific service and the largest asset is usually cash received from services provided.

In your loan proposal package, you'll discuss projected internal cash controls for your business operation. A number of techniques exist to verify that the money collected by your employees makes it to the bank. You should research the various methods used in your industry, or you might construct your own. The idea is that you devise a method that you can demonstrate in your loan proposal package.

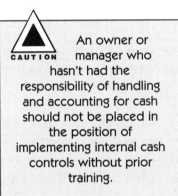

An owner or manager who hasn't had the responsibility of handling and accounting for cash should not be placed in the position of implementing internal cash controls without prior training.

For example, assume that you're proposing to open a restaurant, where cash usually represents a major part of the operation. Typical internal cash control problems that you might encounter are described below (our example is not intended as an indictment against restaurant employees).

In a restaurant operation, cash, checks, and credit cards are received through three principal sources-the waitperson, bartender, and cashier. At the end of the shift, and at the end of the day, every one of these employees must check out and balance the funds they have collected with either you or your manager.

The waitperson is usually issued guest tickets that are numbered and recorded by the issuer. If the tickets are issued in duplicate, the waitperson can give one to the cook, thereby providing the manager with another method of verifying sales. When the waitperson checks out at the end of the shift, the previously issued tickets are either accounted for as blank or as used in a sale.

If the waitperson collects payment directly from the customer, the amount of the total ticket sales is due to you or the manager. If the cashier collects directly from the customer, then you or your manager will check with the cashier to verify the sales of guest tickets issued to the waitperson. As the restaurant owner, you must identify safeguards for handling missing or damaged tickets in the possession of the waitpersons as a means of internal cash control.

Bartenders present a different situation because they usually collect cash for each sale. One way to ensure collection of funds is to have the bartenders issue a cash register receipt to the customer for each order. At the end of the shift, the cash register tape total should match the funds in the cash register, minus the starting bank.

The cashier's tape and register should match every ticket rung up and on hand. You or your manager will be able to verify the tickets through the check out procedures with the waitperson.

At the end of the day, either you or your manager must compare the total guest tickets of each employee with the total amount of money to be deposited in the bank. If the amounts don't match, then your internal cash controls aren't working. Your next step is to retrace the cash and guest ticket trail to find the shortage or overage.

Present and past financial history of company

The present and past financial history of the company should contain the items shown in Table 4.1. However, in new and start-up business situations there is no financial history. Therefore, a projected balance sheet and cash-flow statement will satisfy

note Providing a financial history of the company gives the lender an opportunity to analyze the financial foundation and soundness of your company and its operation.

most of the financial history requirements of a loan proposal package. The lender can determine if: (1) you are making a profit; (2) you are running a sound operation; (3) you have made progress since starting the business; and (4) you can afford to support and repay the loan.

This chapter discusses a year-end balance sheet, projected cash flow, and a profit and loss statement as applicable to start-up businesses. Keep in mind that personal federal tax returns are required for each owner for the last three years.

Balance Sheet

DEFINITION

A *balance sheet* is a financial picture of your company's assets, liabilities, and equity position on a given day. Balance sheets are normally produced either on a monthly basis, known as interim statements, or at the end of your fiscal or calendar year. As a start-up business, you won't have year-end balance sheets for the last three years. Instead this discussion shows you how to prepare an interim statement representing a one-month period.

Let's assume that the following scenario applies to you. You took early retirement and $20,000 in retirement benefits from your management position at a major office supply company and started your own office supply business as a S corporation.

To start your inventory, you borrowed $7,000 against your line of credit and charged $5,000 on your trade account with your distributor for a total inventory value of $15,000. During the month, you sold $30,000 in office and computer-related supplies. You still have an inventory value of $3,000. The company received $25,000 in cash and allowed some customers to establish credit account s representing accounts receivable of $5,000. You use $5,000 of the $25,000 cash generated through sales to apply on your line of credit. You use another $2,500 of the $25,000 to apply on your trade account for the computer equipment purchased through your distributor. You now expended a total of $7,500, leaving you with a cash balance of $17,500.

Almost every business, both small and large, uses a certain dollar figure to determine when they will expense or capitalize a business purchase. Expensing versus capitalizing a purchase requires some thought because your decision will have a tax consequence and affect depreciation.

When you capitalize a purchase, you actually spend the cash and reduce your bank account, but you show the item as an asset to be depreciated over its useful life instead of expensing the full amount at the time of purchase. When you expense a purchase it is not shown as an asset, but as an expense to be deducted from income.

A good figure for a small business to use should be any purchase of $500 and up with a useful life of at least three years. You determine that $500 is an appropriate criterion for your office supply business (i.e., any purchase greater than $500 is capitalized and any purchase less than this amount is expensed, although there are exceptions depending on the useful life and other factors).

> **E-Z TIP**
>
> Talk with your accountant about how to establish appropriate criteria for expensing versus capitalizing that will best serve your operation. This figure will change from time to time depending on your operation and needs.

Of the $20,000 you spent to start the business, you capitalize the full cost of the delivery truck as a fixed asset for $10,500 with a useful life of 36 months. You only used $5,000 of your $20,000 on the truck and the balance for the computer, furniture, and fixtures. You expense the computer for $3,500, and the furniture and fixtures totaling $11,500. Even though the computer equipment, furniture, and fixtures cost more than $500 each, in this example their useful life is not depreciable.

Another item that should appear on the balance sheet is equity position showing owner's draw, capital stock, net profit, and paid in capital. At the end of the month, you (as the owner) draw $2,500 for compensation. Your capital stock is represented by the $20,000 drawn from retirement and used to establish the S corporation and make initial purchases. Your net profit is derived from your profit and loss statement as discussed below.

Now that you have made these decisions and determined how, when, and where to spend your money, you can prepare a projected balance sheet for one month, as shown in Table 4.2.

In preparing your loan proposal package, you must pay attention to financial ratios. Financial ratios are the two most important ratios with regards to government guaranteed loans and are the only ones discussed here. However, in a straight commercial or guaranteed loan the

> *note* The two main ratios that the Small Business Administration and a commercial bank look for in a balance sheet are the current ratio and the debt-to-worth ratio.

lender will probably look at additional ratios. Use standard reference books, such as *Annual Statement Studies* (Robert Morris & Associates, 1997) if you need additional information on ratios and industry standards.

In this balance sheet example, your current assets are $25,500 and your current liabilities are $4,500, for a current ratio of 2.67:1. This means that for every $1 of current debt, you have $2.67 in current assets to cover your debt.

The Small Business Administration and some commercial banks are willing to consider a negative or "minus" current ratio of 1:3 or 1:4. In other words, they would consider a loan when you owe as much as $3 or $4 of current debt for every $1 of current assets.

> ⚠ CAUTION When the current ratio is more than 1:1 and over 1:3 or 1:4, the lender is challenged to take a much closer look at everything in your loan proposal package.

The total debt shown in this balance sheet example is $10,000 and the stockholder's equity (net worth) is $25,708, for a debt-to-worth ratio of 1:2.54. This means that your company has $2.57 of equity for every $1 of debt.

> **note** The Small Business Administration and most commercial banks are willing to look at a debt-to-worth ratio as high as 4:1.

This means your company would owe $4 of debt for every $1 of equity. Again, this ratio will cause the lender to consider your loan proposal request with more scrutiny.

Obviously, a minus ratio in any area of financial reporting is not a good presentation for a loan proposal package. If you can delay your loan request for a few months to correct the situation you would be much better served. If you can't wait, then you should seek help from a consultant or your accountant before you present your loan proposal package.

Try to plan ahead one year for expansion, debt financing, or investment financing that you might require. Begin by keeping track of your company's financial progress on a daily, weekly, and monthly basis. Seek financial counseling if you don't understand the information you receive from your bookkeeper or accountant. Make corrections in your operation that will improve your financial ratios and stability.

Twelve-month cash-flow projection

This cash-flow projection covers a 12-month period beginning with month one and numbered sequentially through 12. Although the previous examples have related to the office supply scenario funded by your retirement benefits, this 12-month cash-flow projection is more complex and is presented for purposes of illustration.

> **note** Cash flow can be simply seen as "money in, money out, and what's left" for a certain period of time, such as one month.

DEFINITION

A *cash-flow projection* is used to determine your future cash needs. Cash flow in this situation determines if there are enough funds available on a regular basis to support your operation.

note

If the "money out" exceeds the "money in," then you have a cash-flow problem. This is a problem because if you start the next period with no funds to carry over from the previous period, and if this trend continues, you may not be in business long.

In order to solve a cash-flow problem, you must invest additional funds in the business to cover the shortage. This investment can be handled by paid in capital, increasing "money in," and/or reducing "money out." In the cash-flow projection, the loan cash injection in the "month one" column keeps the cash on hand shown in the "month two" column positive (Table 4.3).

Profit and loss statement for one month

Let's return to the office supply store scenario and look at your profit and loss statement for the first 30 days of business (Table 4.4). This is not a statement you use to support your loan proposal. Instead, you should use your projected profit and loss statement to help you understand how the statement is developed and how the information from it helps you compile your projected balance sheet.

To calculate your percentage net profit based on your sales, divide the net profit amount ($8,208) by the sales amount ($30,000) and multiply by 100. Your profit and loss statement shows that you made a net profit of 27 percent on sales of $30,000 for one month. Your gross profit ($18,000 divided by $30,000, times 100) is 60 percent of sales, meaning that your cost of sales is 40 percent (not bad). See standard references, such as Robert Morris & Associates (1997) for additional information on industry standards.

note

Whenever your cost-of-sales percentage (40 percent, in this case) is lower than your gross-profit percentage (60 percent), you have more funds available to pay for operating costs, and increased opportunity for improved net profits. What you're looking for here (and, what the lender is looking for) is whether or not this percentage is within the normal range of your industry.

Personal financial statement

The Small Business Administration provides a form for your personal financial information called SBA Standard Form 413-Personal Financial Statement (for additional details see Chapter 5-Preparing Required SBA Forms). The purpose of this information is to provide the lender with information about your personal financial background and stability.

Lenders use your statement to discover other resources available to both you and them. After reviewing your personal financial statement, the lender may either: (1) determine that your personal position is financially sound enough to make the loan based on your loan proposal package; (2) request additional or different collateral for your loan; or (3) determine that you may be too high of a risk for the institution.

If you're not requesting a government-guaranteed loan, you may not be required to use SBA Standard Form 413. Instead, most banks have their own personal financial statement form for you to complete. However, the information requested is almost always consistent regardless of the specific form required. The example shown in Table 4.5 is a generic statement demonstrating typical information expected in a personal financial statement.

> *note* The three types of information requested when applying for a loan are usually related to assets, liabilities, and net worth.

Amount and purpose of loan, use of proceeds, and repayment

This portion of your financial statement should contain clear and concise statements regarding how much money you are requesting, the purpose of the loan, and how you plan to make use of the proceeds. You need to be specific as to each dollar requested. The lender will use this area to determine if your request meets the legal and/or policy requirements of the lending institution. A typical statement addressing these issues is shown in Figure 4.1.

Preparing required SBA forms

Chapter 5

Preparing required SBA forms

What you'll find in this chapter:

- The forms required by the SBA
- Answering the form questions
- Estimated time to complete each form
- What to look for on each form
- Protecting yourself from unreasonable fees

What government application would be complete without massive paperwork? Despite the government's best efforts toward paperwork reduction, paperwork remains essential in preparing your loan proposal package. However, you don't need to fill out every form in existence in order to satisfy the requirements.

 Some of the Small Business Administration forms are required and others are optional or used only for specific purposes.

Our discussion of forms doesn't intend to be comprehensive. Instead, we concentrated on those forms that are essential to your application. Check with your local Small Business Administration office or lender to determine if additional forms are needed as part of your loan proposal package.

Required forms discussed in this chapter include:

- SBA Standard Form 4–Application for Business Loan

- SBA Standard Form 912–Statement of Personal History

- SBA Standard Form 4 Schedule A–Schedule of Collateral, Exhibit A

- SBA Standard Form 413–Personal Financial Statement

- SBA Standard Form 1624–Certification Regarding Debarment, Suspension, Ineligibility and Voluntary Exclusion Lower Tier Covered Transactions

- SBA Standard Form 1846–Statement Regarding Lobbying

- SBA Standard Form 159–Compensation Agreement for Services in Connection with Application and Loan From (or in Participation with) Small /business Administration

Other Small Business Administration forms described in Chapter 6 (*Preparing other SBA forms*) are:

- SBA Standard Form 641–Request for Counseling

- Monthly Cash-flow Projection (formerly SBA Standard Form 1100, also discussed in Chapter 4–Understanding Financial Matters)

- IRS Form 4506–Request for Copy or Transcript of Tax Form

SBA Standard Form 4 – Application for Business Loan

SBA Standard Form 4 is the most important form you'll complete in the loan application process. The Small Business Administration estimates that the burden time for completing this form is 16.8 hours per response—use this information in scheduling time to prepare your loan proposal package.

Keep in mind that an improperly prepared loan application will cause unnecessary delay in the processing of your application. Make sure that you provide every relevant item and that each item will stand up under Small Business Administration scrutiny.

SBA Standard Form 4 consists of six pages—the first four pages, comprising the actual form, are numbered consecutively. The two unnumbered pages consist of a detachable sheet of statements required by law and executive order that you should read and retain (Table 5.1). Your signature indicates that you'll comply with the appropriate government regulations.

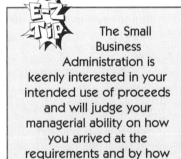

The Small Business Administration is keenly interested in your intended use of proceeds and will judge your managerial ability on how you arrived at the requirements and by how well you present the relevant information.

SBA Standard Form 4, Page 1

Page 1 of the form is divided into four parts:

- Lines 1 through 6 ask for basic information about you and your business (Table 5.2)

- Lines 7 through 13 request information on the use of proceeds (Table 5.3)

- Lines 14 through 17 ask for information on previous Small Business Administration or other federal government debt you incurred

- Lines 18 through 20 request the names of individuals who may have assisted you in preparing the form

After answering questions regarding you and your business (lines 1 through 6), you'll identify how you plan to use the loan amount (lines 7 through 13).

Be sure to enter the gross dollar amounts rounded to the nearest hundreds. Whether the item isn't relevant to your proposed business, either enter "0" or "n/a" for not applicable under the column *"Loan Requested."*

In the next part of the form (lines 14 through 17), you need to indicate if either you or any other principals or affiliates ever requested government financing or are delinquent on the repayment of any federal debt. If applicable, list the following information:

- name of agency

- original amount of loan

- date of request

- approved or declined

- balance

- current or past due

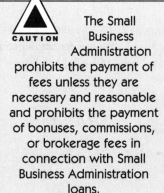

CAUTION The Small Business Administration prohibits the payment of fees unless they are necessary and reasonable and prohibits the payment of bonuses, commissions, or brokerage fees in connection with Small Business Administration loans.

The final information requested on page 1 (lines 18 through 20) is information on the names and occupations of anyone who assisted your in preparing this application. Include the name, occupation, and address of any assistant and the total fees paid and fees due.

If you have questions regarding the range of appropriate fees, contact your local Small Business Administration office for advice. If you do hire someone to assist you in preparing the application, you need to submit SBA Standard Form 159, *"Compensation Agreement for Services in Connection with Application and Loan from (or in Participation with) Small Business Administration,"* discussed later in this chapter.

SBA Standard Form 4, Pages 2 and 3

The top portion of page 2 requests information on business indebtedness and management. Beginning on the bottom portion of the page and continuing onto page 3, are a list of 20 questions and requirements for attachments.

Under business indebtedness, list every installment debt, contract, note, and mortgage payable for each business principal party. If you plan to pay off one or more of these items with the loan proceeds, mark each item with an asterisk and be prepared to present a full explanation for the reason you've included the debt. If you need more space, attach a separate sheet.

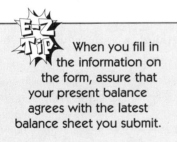

When you fill in the information on the form, assure that your present balance agrees with the latest balance sheet you submit.

The section on management is relevant to the proprietor, partners, officers, and directors who hold outstanding stock (show 100 percent of ownership). The requested information and comments are shown in Table 5.4. Attach a separate sheet if needed.

The balance of the form consists of 20 questions—be sure that you address each question and provide the required exhibits. The compilation of each exhibit is one reason you can expect to spend nearly 20 hours preparing this form. The exhibits are identified as Exhibits A through O and you must sign and date each one that you prepare. The 20 questions are shown in Table 5.5 along with comments.

SBA Standard Form 4, Page 4

Page 4 is the applicant's certification signature page. Your signature certifies that you have read and received a copy of the statements required by law and executive order, and that you agree to comply with the appropriate limitations of the notice and any other requirements. Each proprietor, general partner, limited partner, or stockholder owning 20 percent or more and each guarantor must sign the form (each person should only sign once).

SBA Standard Form 912 – Statement of Personal History

SBA Standard Form 912 is a statement of personal history required for each member of the business requesting assistance and must be submitted in triplicate with the Small Business Administration loan application. Small Business Administration estimates the burden time per response for completing the form is 15 minutes. Individuals who are required to submit this form include:

- the proprietor, if the company is a sole proprietorship

- each partner if the company is a partnership

- each officer, director, and each holder of 20 percent or more of the voting stock, if the company is a corporation

- any other person, including a hired manager, who has authority to speak for and commit the borrower in the management of the business

SBA Standard Form 4 Schedule A – Schedule of Collateral, Exhibit A

DEFINITION

The assets that you and the other owners provide to the lender as security for a loan is the *collateral*. Use SBA Standard Form 4 Schedule A to itemize the collateral that you and the other owners are planning to offer. Take the time to carefully prepare this form—the Small Business Administration and your bank will scrutinize your proposed collateral, which may include one or more of the following:

- mortgages on buildings or equipment

- chattel mortgages on your vehicle or other items of value (in some states, instead of chattel mortgages, you must conform to the uniform consumer credit code)

- inventory receipts for saleable merchandise (but only when the inventory is maintained in a bonded or acceptable warehouse or storage area)

- personal guarantees or endorsements (and sometimes current receivables)

This form consists of two pages. The first page begins with basic information identifying the applicant, followed by *"Section I-Real Estate."* The second page contains *"Section II-Personal Property"* and a place for your signature. The information requested on the form and comments are listed in Table 5.7.

SBA Standard Form 413 – Personal Financial Statement

SBA Standard Form 413 is designed to present information regarding your personal financial situation and other information that's important to the

Keep in mind that if you fill out the SBA *Personal Financial Statement*, you'll be able to transfer the information to any other form requiring personal financial information.

lender. Use of this particular form may not be mandatory, although you must present the same information in one format or another as required by the lender.

SBA estimates that the average burden time for completing this form is 1.5 hours per response. Individuals who are required to complete this form include:

- each owner

- each limited partner owning 20 percent or more interest

- each general partner

- each stockholder owning 20 percent or more of the voting stock

- each corporate officer and director

- any other person or entity providing a guarantee on the loan

This form consists of two pages divided into eight sections. The information requested on the form and comments are shown on Table 5.8. For additional discussions of SBA Standard Form 413 and related financial matters, see Chapter 4 (Understanding Financial Matters).

SBA Standard Form 1624 – Certification Regarding Debarment, Suspension, Ineligibility and Voluntary Exclusion Lower Tier Covered Transactions

This certification is required by the regulations implementing Executive Order 12549, Debarment and Suspension, 13 C.F.R. Part 142. The purpose of this form is to assure that you and/or your company's principles aren't prohibited from participation in this transaction by any federal department or agency resulting from either debarment, suspension, proposed for debarment, declared ineligibility, or voluntary exclusion.

The instructions are printed on the back of the form and you should read them carefully before you sign the form. Refer to Table 5.9 for the plain language translation of each instruction. If you're unable to certify to any of the statements presented on this form, prepare a written explanation and attach it to the loan application.

SBA Standard Form 1846 – Statement Regarding Lobbying

The statement regarding lobbying is a statement for loan guarantees and loan insurance assuring that you have not paid funds to any person to influence decisions regarding your loan application. That is, you aren't allowed to lobby any federal employee or elected official. However, if you have lobbied anyone, you're requested to complete and submit SBA Standard Form LLL, *"Disclosure of Lobbying Activities."* Details and comments on this form are shown in Table 5.7. The Small Business Administration doesn't provide an estimate of burden time for completing this form, although you can expect to complete the form in a few minutes.

SBA Standard Form 159 – Compensation Agreement for Services in Connection with Application and Loan From (or in Participation with) Small Business Administration

The Small Business Administration doesn't require that you have a representative when you apply for a loan, although sometimes loan applicants need assistance from professionals, consultants, or others. Realistically, you may need help from an accountant in preparing financial statements or from an attorney at the time the loan is closed.

In seeking legitimate representation, find individuals or firms who are going to charge you reasonable fees for needed services. Avoid representatives who may request a percentage of the loan amount as compensation or who require payment of either a bonus, brokerage fee, or commission, as this is prohibited by the Small Business Administration.

Be alert to individuals or firms claiming to be "authorized representatives" of the Small Business Administration—there are no such representatives.

To protect yourself from unreasonable fees or other charges, use SBA Standard Form 159, *"Compensation Agreement for Services in Connection with Application and Loan from (or in Participation with) Small Business Administration,"* to identify any representative you may have hired. If you have questions about what constitutes a reasonable fee, contact your Regional or Field Office.

The Small Business Administration estimates the time required to complete this form is six hours, although this seems excessive. A more realistic estimate is probably one hour or less per response. Refer to policy and regulations concerning representatives and their fees in Table 5.11 and to form instructions in Table 5.12.

Preparing other SBA forms

Chapter 6

Preparing other SBA forms

The Small Business Administration offers a number of other forms or guidelines and instructions that you may need in preparing your loan application. SBA Standard Form 641 is a request for counseling, followed by instructions and guidelines for preparing a monthly cash-flow projection sheet (formerly SBA Standard Form 1100). The final form discussed in this section is IRS Standard Form 4506 for requesting a copy or transcript of your tax forms.

SBA Standard Form 641 – Request for Counseling

If you need assistance, the Small Business Administration offers technical and management help free of charge. Make your request using SBA Standard Form 641 and submit the form in triplicate to your Small Business

Administration office (Table 6.1). If you prefer, you can register on-line at *http://www.sbaonline.SBA.gov/textonly/shareware*. The Small Business Administration estimates that this form requires seven minutes per response.

Monthly Cash-flow Projection or Equivalent Form (Formerly SBA Standard Form 1100)

A monthly cash-flow projection is essential in business planning and offers numerous benefits to the small business owner. As a business start-up, you'll not have a track record with which to develop your plan and may have to rely on industry averages to develop your projection.

A cash-flow projection asks several basic questions regarding your money on a monthly basis:

- how much you have to start the period

- how much will be received during the period

- how much will be paid out during the period

- how much will you have at the end of the period

note Monthly cash-flow projections may be prepared a number of ways, including specific software applications developed for small businesses.

Although the Small Business Administration no longer uses SBA Standard Form 1100, a 12-month minimum cash flow is still required. The following two tables (Tables 6.2 and 6.3) provide the necessary information that must be included in your cash-flow projection. You should use the information in these tables as a guide when you create your own cash-flow format.

The Small Business Administration estimated the burden time for each response is one hour. However, development of a cash-flow projection can require more time, depending on your familiarity with cash-flow projections and spread sheets; and on your skills at estimating costs and revenues.

SBA Standard Form 4506 – Request for Copy or Transcript of Tax Form

The lender will want to see your tax returns for the past one to three years to confirm that you filed with the Internal Revenue Service and that the information is the same as what you provided the lender. Another reason might be verifying that you didn't claim any itemized deductions for a residence. In addition to your personal and business tax IRS returns (as applicable), they may ask for more information.

A transcript is all you need to provide to the lender and is the recommended choice. If you order a copy of your records, you may wait months for a response. As a practical matter, order a transcript first. The disadvantage to a transcript is that the document doesn't reflect any changes that either you or the IRS may have made to the original return.

Although the Small Business Administration doesn't provide a burden time for completing a response, plan for about an hour. Instructions for this form are shown in Table 6.4 and specific items and explanations are listed on Table 6.5.

Compiling your loan package

7

Chapter 7

Compiling your loan package

Now that you have prepared your narratives, completed your forms, and gathered your supporting documents and other attachments, you should be ready to compile your loan proposal package. However, before you assemble and bind your package, it's a good idea to spend time correcting your package and applying rules of thumb for reader-friendly writing. Next, you should devote some time to polishing your package and looking good. These activities give your package a professional and organized appearance that make a positive first impression.

Correcting your package

The three most important steps in making corrections are (1) proofread, (2) proofread, and (3) proofread. Do this for each part of your package, including the forms, or have someone else proofread for you. Look at both the hard copy and electronic version of each part—you tend to find different errors for each medium. Your spell-check will not find every mistake and a single letter can make a difference in the message. An international company prepared a proposal for a Native American group. The "t" was dropped from the word "Native," giving new meaning to the group, "Naive American."

A graduate student submitted a proposal to study low-income families. When referring to "poor" people, the student accidentally substituted a "p" for the "r" in the word "poor," resulting in an unflattering description.

 Errors can have a negative impact on the individual who reviews your loan proposal package. Hand-written corrections will not impress the lender either.

 For the narrative, read each individual word out loud to either yourself or someone else. Any sentences that sound awkward probably are. Don't depend on your software to find every error—this will not happen.

 For the financial part of your loan proposal package, double-check each figure. You want to demonstrate competence with numbers and would be embarrassed to have the lender find mathematical errors.

Applying rules of thumb for reader-friendly writing

Applying the following basic rules for reader-friendly writing usually makes the reader's job easier. Attention to white space, paragraph and sentence length, bulleted and numbered lists, font and point size, and emphasis impact the lender's impression of your package. You might also want to incorporate these rules into your other written projects and see how much they improve the reader's receptivity to your ideas.

- **White space**-A page that's overflowing with text discourages readers—leave plenty of white space and use 1-inch top and bottom margins and 1.25-inch left and right margins. If space allows, try preparing your documents using a line spacing of 1.5.

- **Paragraph length**-Your shortest paragraph should consist of two complete sentences. Each paragraph should be a maximum of nine lines in length—better to have two short paragraphs of five lines each than a single long paragraph that isn't read. Remember, the word "paragraph" has nine letters.

- **Sentence length**-Average sentences should be about 15 words in length—range can be from 10 to 20 words. Only lawyers write sentences in the 60+ range! Sentences consisting of nine words or less are considered simplistic. Conveniently, the phrase "sentence length" has 15 characters.

- **Bulleted or numbered lists**-Readers are automatically drawn to bulleted and numbered lists when browsing through a document—use this to your advantage.

When preparing a list, select only the most important material and try to limit each list to a maximum of six items. If you have more than six items in a list, you can probably develop two lists each

> Itemize with bulleted lists whenever the order of the items isn't important. If the order is important, use numbered lists.

containing related items. Limit yourself to one list per page, if possible, and no more than two.

- **Avoid "cute" bullets**-bankers are conservative, so use dots for your bulleted lists and save the fancy bullets for your marketing efforts. For numbered lists, use conventional sequential numbers followed by periods (e.g., "1."). Avoid dividing a list by inserting a subordinate list under an item—this isn't a reader-friendly technique (i.e., don't put lists inside of other lists).

- **Font and point size**-Choose fonts that are easy on the eye. When writing narratives, Times New Roman (a serif font) is easier for North Americans to read than Arial (a sans serif font). However, European readers an more accustomed to san serif fonts. For lenders with bifocals, text smaller than 11 is a challenge—use 12 whenever possible.

You can use more than one font in a document, to emphasize section headings for example. However, using more than three is distracting to the reader. Two fonts per document are the easiest on the reader—use one in the section headings and the other in the text. Notice that this text uses Times New Roman, with Castle T font for chapter headings and Arial Narrow for tables and figures. A distinctly different font was chosen for tables and figures so that the reader would always have a visual signal regarding the type of material presented.

- **Emphasis**-READING TEXT IN CAPS IS HARD ON THE EYE AND READERS TEND TO SKIP TEXT IN CAPS, ESPECIALLY IF IT'S LENGTHY. The same is true for italics—readers will skip text in italics. The reader is likely to overlook information that's emphasized by an underline. If you want to emphasize something in your text, highlight it in bold rather than with caps, italics, or underline. The reader's eye is automatically drawn to text in bold.

Polishing your package

Now that you have corrected your package and applied your rules for reader-friendly writing, you're ready to polish the package. Using headers in the narrative sections of your package will look professional, although it will not be practical to insert headers onto the forms.

Organize your material for presentation. Including a table of contents allows the reviewer to quickly find the portions of the package of greatest interest. Depending upon how you choose to group your material, you may or may not elect to add page numbers to individual sections.

Headers

When you set up the page for the narratives, include a header. This adds a professional touch to your package and prevents a disaster in the event you package is disassembled and accidentally mixed with another. Typical information appearing in the header includes:

- your company name

- location (city and state)

- date

- reference to "SBA Loan Proposal Package"

Organization

Lenders assume that you know how to organize your package for presentation and, generally speaking, a lender doesn't provide guidelines on content or order of presentation.

E-Z TIP: If your package is missing something, or the lender can't find pertinent items, your application may be rejected. Therefore, organize your package carefully and provide a table of contents.

Because you have narrative materials, forms, and other supporting documents or attachments, numbered sections are a convenient way to organize the material. Use die-cut numbered tabs available from your local office supply store for each copy of the document you intend to bind. Group similar materials together and assign numbered sections to each. One method for grouping the contents is shown in Table 7.1. Notice that the materials aren't necessarily grouped in the same order in which they were prepared.

Looking good

A loan proposal package is, in effect, a marketing document. The objective is to assure that the image your package projects reflects on you as a responsible and well-organized business person. Once you have decided on the image that you wish to project, you'll need to determine the means of reproduction, assembling, and binding.

> **E-Z TIP** Remember that your audience (the lender) probably has a conservative viewpoint and will be most comfortable with a conservative presentation.

First impressions are lasting and you want to make a good impression on the lender. Bankers are human beings, too, and respond to aesthetics—a well-presented package is more pleasing than a sloppy one and may be the first indication the lender has of your organizational and managerial abilities.

Looking good doesn't need to be an expensive endeavor. In today's world of desktop publishing, a number of companies produce a variety of affordable quality paper products. Check your local business supply store and select a paper that helps promote your image as a competent business person.

Be conservative when selecting a paper product. Save your imagination and flash for your marketing. If your package is too flashy, the lender might see your effort as frivolous and lacking in good sense. When selecting a paper, think in terms of weight and color.

> **E-Z TIP** Generally, higher-weight paper is preferable to lower-weight paper— heavier paper is "richer" and projects importance.

White paper is a perennial favorite in the business world and white paper with black ink has high contrast, making it a reader-friendly combination. Suitable color choices and the images they project are listed in Table 7.2.

Design and prepare a cover for your loan proposal package (an example is shown in Figure 7.1). Select a heavy stock for your cover in an appropriate color that complements your paper and use the same stock for the back cover. Include the following information on your front cover:

- your company name

- package description

- name of the financial institution

- name of the individual receiving the package

- name of the organization and the individual submitting the package

- name, address, and telephone numbers of the organization or individual preparing the package

Reproduction

Now that you selected your paper and heavy stock for the front and back covers, you're ready to reproduce your document. Plan to prepare one complete loan package original and a number of complete photocopy reproductions.

> *note*
> You'll need one original loan proposal package and several reproductions for the lender, and several for yourself.

Print your loan proposal package in black ink—colored ink will not copy clearly when you make reproductions. If you selected a textured paper, print and reproduction copy quality may be poor, especially for small print used on many of the forms. If you included color photographs, you may want to reproduce these on a color photocopy machine for insertion into your loan package original and reproductions.

The items you should include in your loan package original and reproductions, the method of preparation, and the recommenced materials are shown in Tables 7.3 and 7.4.

Assembling and binding

By now, you should have the following:

- complete loan package original (compiled in the order of presentation)

- complete loan package reproductions (compiled in the order of presentation)

- numbered tabs

Your next job is to be sure that the loan package original and each reproduction are assembled in the correct order. Use your table of contents and numbered tabs to compile the loan package items and double check that each package has the same contents and items assembled in the same order.

Binding is the final touch. Three-ring binders and comb binding are two popular methods, although you can check with your local office supply store or photocopy shop for other binding options. Generally, binders are acceptable, although the pages are prone to tear out—a major disadvantage. Additionally, binders are easily disassembled and someone may remove a section and not return it.

 A comb binding is a choice that works well for loan package submission because it's less likely to lose sheets or sections than a binder. If you choose a comb binding, be sure to protect your front and back cover pages with heavy plastic sheets. The disadvantage to the comb binding is that adding material to the package after the binding is completed is difficult.

About BIC's information center

Chapter 8

About BIC's information center

What you'll find in this chapter:

- ➡ An introduction to the BIC
- ➡ What's available at the BIC resource center
- ➡ About SCORE counseling services
- ➡ The facts about the SBDC program
- ➡ How to contact a SBDC center near you

The information superhighway contains many "toll-booths." The purchase of computers and software can be too costly for new entrepreneurs or others who are just getting by. Fortunately, you may avoid these problems by turning to the Small Business Association's (SBA's) high-tech, state-of-the-art, multi-media Business Information Center (BIC), located in Denver, Colorado. SBA's BIC is an interactive business reference library providing one-stop shopping for a variety of business-related topics that help you start a new business and make it succeed.

BIC's reference library has over 500 books, manuals, and videos on how to start and grow a business. In most cases these reference materials offer step-by-step, hands-on instructions about specific business topics ranging from starting an ad agency to women apparel shops. It offers help on how to develop a comprehensive business plan, effective marketing plan, cash-flow statement, and even designing your own effective business cards. BIC clients have access to the Internet and SBA's Internet home page which can be found at *http://www.sba.gov*. It contains over 500 downloadable business development files which can be accessed at the BIC or on your own home computer.

In addition to its expansive reference library, the BIC offers state-of-the-art, user-friendly personal computers, graphic work stations, CD-ROM technology, Microsoft Office 97 programs and accessories, census data, and tax return preparation software. Clients have access to IBM, Compaq, and Apple Computers. Afraid to surf the internet alone? BIC has on-site counseling provided by Counselors to America's Small Business (SCORE), who guide you safely onto the Information Superhighway and show you interesting links to business success. They can assist in getting your business into the SBA's Pro-Net marketing program. These former business professionals lend their tried and tested experience and know-how to assist clients who confront starting, operating, and growing a small business issues. Counseling is free and available by appointment.

The success of your business

SBA and SCORE established the Denver BIC as a state-of-the-art facility containing a library of publication, video, and audio reference material and seven computer stations loaded with business applications software, equipped with CD-ROM drives, and telephone interface BIC is staffed by a full-time SBA manager, assisted by specially trained SCORE volunteers.

Publication library

An important element of the library is the set of guides compiled by *Entrepreneur Magazine*. These guides provide information on start-up costs, location facilities, inventory, and marketing for 186 businesses. A set of 50 volumes from Oasis Press provides information on starting and operating a business in the 50 states of the United States. Other volumes in the library cover the subjects of business plan preparation, handbooks and guides, marketing, finance, personnel, and specialty, home-based and women-owned businesses.

Video/audio library

The publication library is complemented by an extensive collection of video and audio cassettes, many of them prepared by INC Magazine. These cassettes, which cover many of the same topics as the publication library, enhance the learning experience by providing alternatives to hard copy print media. The cassette players are equipped with headsets to eliminate interference with other BIC users. See Table 8 for a list of typical BIC videos.

Computer facility

IBM-compatible personal computers are available. Although these computers are not networked, they are linked to a wide-carriage dot-matrix printer and a laser printer. Multimedia equipment supplied with each computer includes an internal CD-ROM drive, a 16-bit sound card, external speakers, and a headset.

Each computer is also equipped with a modem which provides access to computer bulletin boards, the Internet, the Library of Congress, FAX, and the on-line catalogs of over 200 libraries in the U.S. using the Colorado CARL and ACLIN systems.

The computer operating systems include DOS and Windows. The Windows application programs loaded in each computer include the Microsoft Office Suite, Microsoft Publisher, and Microsoft Office Assistant. The Bookshelf program provides easy access to standard reference books such as a dictionary, atlas, encyclopedia and thesaurus. Another special application program allows the user to print business cards an forms such as invoices, bills of lading, and past-due notices.

The CD-ROM database includes U.S. census data, economic data, and Dunn & Bradstreet information. A set of 5 CDs allows the user to have access to 85 million business and residential telephone listings from white and yellow page directories across the country. General information is available from Encarta, an interactive multimedia encyclopedia containing 26,000 articles.

SCORE counseling

Service Corps of Retired Executives (SCORE) is a program of the Small Business Administration comprised of business executives who volunteer their time to share their management and technical expertise with present and prospective owners and managers of small businesses. Every effort is made to match a client's need with a counselor who is experience in that line of business. Counseling is provided without charge to the client and is confidential.

SCORE workshops

Workshops of interest to entrepreneurs are presented each month for a nominal charge. These include:

1) how to really start your own business

2) structuring your business

3) marketing/advertising/salesmanship

4) how to write a business plan

SCORE business information directory

Entrepreneurs who want to start a business, or improve the performance of an existing one, need information to meet this goal. Denver SCORE Chapter 62 discovered that a great deal of information was available on a number of SBA computerized bulletin boards.

To make the bulletin board information available to entrepreneurs, SCORE Chapter 62 decided to act as an intermediary. The contents of the bulletin boards were reviewed and files downloaded to a computerized database. The files were then grouped by topic (Accounting to Writing). The copyrighted *"Business Information Directory"* consolidates the files according to topic. The Directory was prepared to provide a method for clients to order the topics in accordance with instructions in the directory. SCORE Chapter 62 then provides the chosen files to the users on a floppy disk at a charge of $2.00 per file. The directory itself costs $10.00

Facts about the Small Business Development Center program

The U.S. Small Business Administration administers the Small Business Development Center (SBDC) program to provide management assistance to current and prospective small business owners. SBDCs offer one-stop assistance to small businesses by providing a wide variety of information and guidance in central and easily accessible branch locations.

The program is a cooperative effort of the private sector, the educational community, and federal, state and local governments. It enhances economic development by providing small businesses with management and technical assistance.

There are now 70 Small Business Development Centers—one in every state (Texas and California have six), the District of Columbia, Puerto Rico, the U.S. Virgin Islands and Guam—with a network of more than 950 service locations. In each state there is a lead organization that sponsors the SBDC and manages the program. The lead organization coordinates program services offered to small businesses through a network of subcenters and satellite locations in each state. Subcenters are located at colleges, universities, community colleges, vocational schools, chambers of commerce and economic development corporations.

SBDC assistance is tailored to the local community and the needs of individual clients. Each center develops services in cooperation with local SBA district offices to ensure statewide coordination with other available resources. Each center has a director, staff members, volunteers and part-time personnel. Qualified individuals recruited from professional and trade associations, the legal and banking communities, academia, chambers of commerce, and Service Corps of Retired Executives (SCORE) are among those who donate their services. SBDCs also use paid consultants, consulting engineers and testing laboratories from the private sector to help clients who need specialized expertise.

What the program does

The SBDC Program is designed to deliver up-to-date counseling, training and technical assistance in all aspects of small business management. SBDC services include, but are not limited to, assisting small businesses with financial, marketing, production, organization, engineering and technical problems, and feasibility studies. Special SBDC programs and economic development activities include international trade assistance, technical assistance, procurement assistance, venture-capital formation and rural development.

SBDCs also make special efforts to reach socially and economically disadvantaged groups, veterans, women and the disabled. Assistance is provided to current and potential small business owners. SBDCs also provide assistance to small businesses applying for Small Business Innovation and Research grants from federal agencies.

Eligibility

SBDC assistance is available to anyone interested in starting or expanding a small business that cannot afford the services of a private consultant.

Lead SBDCs

- University of Alabama, Birmingham, AL (205) 934-7260

- University of Alaska/Anchorage, Anchorage, AK (907) 274-7232

- Maricopa County Community College, Tempe, AZ (602) 731-8720

- University of Arkansas, Little Rock, AR (501) 324-9043

- California Trade and Commerce Agency, Sacramento, CA (916) 324-5068

- Colorado Office of Business Development, Denver, CO (303) 892-3809

- University of Connecticut, Storrs, CT (203) 486-4135

- University of Delaware, Newark, DE (302) 831-2747

- Howard University, Washington, DC (202) 806-1550

- University of West Florida, Pensacola, FL (904) 444-2060

- University of Georgia, Athens, GA (706) 542-6762

- University of Guam, Mangilao, GU (671) 735-2590

- University of Hawaii at Hilo, Hilo, HI (808) 933-3515

- Boise State University, Boise, ID (208) 385-1640

- Department of Commerce and Community Affairs, Springfield, IL (217) 524-5856

- Economic Development Council, Indianapolis, IN (317) 264-6871

- Iowa State University, Ames, IA (515) 292-6351

- Fort Hays State University, Hay, KS (913) 628-6786 or 5340

- University of Kentucky, Lexington, KY (606) 257-7668

- Northeast Louisiana University, Monroe, LA (318) 342-5506

- University of Southern Maine, Portland, ME (207) 780-4420

- Department of Economic and Employment Development, Baltimore, MD (410) 333-6995

- University of Massachusetts, Amherst, MA (413) 545-6301

- Wayne State University, Detroit, MI (313) 964-1798 Department of Trade and Economic Development, St. Paul, MN (612) 297-5770

- University of Mississippi, University, MS (601) 232-5001

- University of Missouri, Columbia, MO (314) 882-0344

- Department of Commerce, Helena, MT (406) 444-4780

- University of Nebraska at Omaha, Omaha, NE (402) 554-2521

- University of Nevada in Reno, Reno, NV (702) 784-1717

- University of New Hampshire, Durham, NH (603) 862-2200

- Rutgers University, Newark, NJ (201) 648-5950

- Santa Fe Community College, Santa Fe, NM (505) 438-1362

- State University of New York, Albany, NY (518) 443-5398

- University of North Carolina, Raleigh, NC (919) 715-7272

- University of North Dakota, Grand Forks, ND (701) 777-3700

- Department of Development, Columbus, OH (614) 466-2711

- Southeastern Oklahoma State University, Durant, OK (405) 924-0277

- Lane Community College, Eugene, OR (503) 726-2250

- University of Pennsylvania, Philadelphia, PA (215) 898-1219

- University of Puerto Rico, San Juan, PR (787) 250-0000 Ext. 2072

- Bryant College, Smithfield, RI (401) 2 3 2 -6111

- University of South Carolina, Columbia, SC (803) 777-4907

- University of South Dakota, Vermillion, SD (605) 677-5498

- University of Memphis, Memphis, TN (901) 678-2500

- Dallas County Community College, Dallas, TX (214) 860-5833

- University of Houston, Houston, TX (713) 752-8444

- Texas Tech University, Lubbock, TX (806) 745-3973

- University of Texas at San Antonio, San Antonio, TX (210) 558-2450

- Salt Lake City Community College, Sandy, UT (801) 255-5878

- Vermont Technical College, Randolph Center, VT (802) 728-9101

- University of the Virgin Islands, St. Thomas, VI (809) 776-3206

- Department of Economic Development, Richmond, VA (804) 371-8258

- Washington State University, Pullman, WA (509) 335-1576

- West Virginia Development Office, Charleston, WV (304) 558-2960

- University of Wisconsin, Madison, WI (608) 263-7794

- University of Wyoming, Laramie WY (307) 766-3505

Funding

The SBA provides 50 percent or less of the operating funds for each state SBDC. One or more sponsors provide the rest. These matching-fund contributions are provided by state legislatures, private-sector foundations and grants, state and local chambers of commerce, state-chartered economic-development corporations, public and private universities, vocational and technical schools, community colleges, etc. Increasingly, sponsors' contributions exceed the minimum 50 percent matching share.

For more information

Information is power. Make it your business to know what is available, where to get it and, most importantly, how to use it. Sources of information include U.S. Small Business Administration:

- SBA District Offices

- Small Business Development Centers (SBDC)

- Service Corps of Retired Executives (SCORE)

- SBA On-line (electronic bulletin board)

- Business Information Centers (BICs)

The SBA has offices located throughout the United States. For the one nearest you, look under "*U.S. Government*" in your telephone directory, or call the SBA Answer Desk at (800) 8-ASK-SBA (827-5722). To send a fax to the SBA, dial (202) 205-7064. For the hearing impaired, the TDD number is (704) 344-6640.

To access the agency's electronic public information services, you may call the following SBA On-line (electronic bulletin board, modem and computer required):

- (800) 697-4636 (limited access)

- (900) 463-4636 (full access)

- (202) 401-9600 (D.C. metro area)

Internet (using uniform resource locators [URLs]):

- SBA Home Page: http://www.sba.gov

- SBA gopher: gopher://gopher.sba.gov

- File transfer protocol: ftp://ftp.sba.gov

- Telnet: telnet://sbaonline.sba.gov

- U.S. Business Advisor: http://www.business.gov

You also may request a free copy of The Resource Directory for Small Business Management, a listing of for sale publications and videotapes, from your local SBA office or the SBA Answer Desk.

Other Sources

- state economic development agencies

- chambers of commerce

- local colleges and universities

- libraries

- manufacturers and suppliers of small business products and services

- small business or industry trade associations

All of the SBA's programs and services are provided to the public on a nondiscriminatory basis.

The forms in this guide

NOTE: The forms in this guide were current at the time of
publication. To view and download revised forms from our web
site at: **www.MadeE-Z.com**

U.S. Small Business Administration

APPLICATION FOR BUSINESS LOAN

Individual	Full Address

Name of Applicant Business	Tax I.D. No. or SSN

Full Street Address of Business	Tel. No. (inc. A/C)

City	County	State	Zip	Number of Employees (including subsidiaries and affiliates)
Type of Business		Date Business Established		At Time of Application
Bank of Business Account and Address				If Loan is Approved
				Subsidiaries or Affiliates (Separate from above)

Use of Proceeds: (Enter Gross Dollar Amounts Rounded to the Nearest Hundreds)	Loan Requested		Loan Requested
Land Acquisition		Payoff SBA Loan	
New Construction/ Expansion Repair		Payoff Bank Loan (Non SBA Associated)	
Acquisition and/or Repair of Machinery and Equipment		Other Debt Payment (Non SBA Associated	
Inventory Purchase		All Other	
Working Capital (Including Accounts Payable		Total Loan Requested	
Acquisition of Existing Business		Term of Loan - (Requested Mat.)	___ Yrs.

PREVIOUS SBA OR OTHER FEDERAL GOVERNMENT DEBT: If you or any principals or affiliates have 1) ever requested Government Financing or 2) are delinquent on the repayment of any Federal Debt complete the following:

Name of Agency	Original Amount of Loan	Date of Request	Approved or Declined	Balance	Current or Past Due
	$			$	
	$			$	

ASSISTANCE   List the names(s) and occupations of any who assisted in the preparation of this form, other than the applicant.

Name and Occupation	Address	Total Fees Paid	Fees Due
Name and Occupation	Address	Total Fees Paid	Fees Due

PLEASE NOTE: The estimated burden hours for the completion of this form is 19.8 hours per response. If you have any questions or comments concerning this estimate or any other aspect of this information collection please contact, Chief Administrative Information Branch, U.S. Small Business Administration, Washington, D.C. 20416 and Gary Waxman, Clearance Officer, Paperwork Reduction Project (3745-0016), Office of Management and Budget, Washington, D.C. 20503.

SBA Form 4 (5-92) Previous Edition is Obsolete

ALL EXHIBITS MUST BE SIGNED AND DATED BY PERSON SIGNING THIS FORM

BUSINESS INDEBTEDNESS: Furnish the following information on all installment debts, contracts, notes, and mortgages payable. Indicate by an asterisk(*) items to be paid by loan proceeds and reason for paying same (present balance should agree with the latest balance sheet submitted).

To Whom Payable	Original Amount	Original Date	Present Balance	Rate of Interest	Maturity Date	Monthly Payment	Security	Current or Past Due
Acct. #	$		$			$		
Acct. #	$		$			$		
Acct. #	$		$			$		
Acct. #	$		$			$		

MANAGEMENT (Proprietor, partners, officers, directors all holders of outstanding stock - **100% of ownership must be shown**). Use separate sheet if necessary.

Name and Social Security Number and Position Title	Complete Address	% Owned	*Military Service From	To	*Race	*Sex

*This data is collected for statistical purpose only. It has no bearing on the credit decision to approve or decline this application.

THE FOLLOWING EXHIBITS MUST BE COMPLETED WHERE APPLICABLE. ALL QUESTIONS ANSWERED ARE MADE A PART OF THE APPLICATION.

For Guaranty Loans please provide an original and one copy (Photocopy is Acceptable) of the Application Form, and all Exhibits to the participating lender. For Direct Loans submit one original copy of the application and Exhibits to SBA.

1. Submit SBA Form 912 (Personal History Statement) for each person e.g. owners, partners, officers, directors, major stockholders, etc.; the instructions are on SBA Form 912.

2. If you collateral consists of (A) Land and Building, (B) Machinery and Equipment, (C) Furniture and Fixtures, (D) Accounts Receivable, (E) Inventory, (F) Other, please provide an itemized list (labeled Exhibit A) that contains serial and identification numbers for all articles that had an original value greater than $500. Include a legal description of Real Estate offered as collateral.

3. Furnish a signed current personal balance sheet (SBA Form 413 may be used for this purpose) for each stockholder (with 20% or greater ownership), partner, officer and owner. Social Security number should be included on personal financial statement. It should be as of the same date as the most recent business financial statements. Label the Exhibit B.

4. Include the statements listed below: 1,2,3 for the last three years; also 1,2,3,4 as of the same date, which are current within 90 days of filing the application; and statement 5, if applicable. This is Exhibit C (SBA has Management Aids that help in the preparation of financial statements.) All information must be **signed and dated**.

1. Balance Sheet   2. Profit and Loss Statement
3. Reconciliation of Net Worth
4. Aging of Accounts Receivable and Payable
5. Earnings projects for at least one year where financial statements for the last three years are unavailable or where requested by District Office.
    (If Profit and Loss Statement is not available, explain why and substitute Federal Income Tax Forms.)

5. Provide a brief history of your company and a paragraph describing the expected benefits it will receive from the loan. Label it Exhibit D.

6. Provide a brief description similar to a resume of the education, technical and business background for all the people listed under Management. Please mark it Exhibit E.

ALL EXHIBITS MUST BE SIGNED AND DATED BY PERSON SIGNING THIS FORM

7. Do you have any co-signers and/or guarantors for this loan? If so, please submit their names, addresses, tax id Numbers, and current personal balance sheet(s) as Exhibit F.

8. Are you buying machinery or equipment with your loan money? If so, you must include a list of equipment and cost as quoted by the seller and his name and address. This is Exhibit G.

9. Have you or any officer of your company ever been involved in bankruptcy or insolvency proceedings? If so, please provide the details as Exhibit H. If none, check here: ☐Yes ☐No

10. Are you or your business involved in any pending lawsuits? If yes, provide the details as Exhibit I. If none, check here: ☐Yes ☐No

11. Do you or your spouse or any member of your household, or anyone who owns, manages, or directs your business or their spouses or members of their households work for the Small Business Administration, Small Business Advisory Council, SCORE or ACE, any Federal Agency, or the participating lender? If so, please provide the name and address of the person and the office where employed. Label this Exhibit J. If none, check here: ☐Yes ☐No

12. Does your business, its owners or majority stockholders own or have a controlling interest in other businesses? If yes, please provide their names and the relationship with your company along with a current balance sheet and operating statement for each. This should be Exhibit K.

13. Do you buy from, sell to, or use the services of any concern in which someone in your company has a significant financial interest? If yes, provide details on a separate sheet of paper labeled Exhibit L.

14. If your business is a franchise, include a copy of the franchise agreement and a copy of the FTC disclosure statement supplied to you by the Franchisor. Please include it as Exhibit M.

CONSTRUCTION LOANS ONLY

15. Include a separate exhibit (Exhibit N) the estimated cost of the project and a statement of the source of any additional funds.

16. Provide copies of preliminary construction plans and specifications. Include them as Exhibit O. Final plans will be required prior to disbursement.

DIRECT LOANS ONLY

17. Include two bank declination letters with your application. (In cities with 200,000 people or less, one letter will be sufficient.) These letters should include the name and telephone number of the persons contacted at the banks, the amount and terms of the loan, the reason for decline and whether or not the bank will participate with SBA.

EXPORT LOANS

18. Does your business presently engage in Export Trade? Check here: ☐Yes ☐No

19. Do you have plans to begin exporting as a result of this loan? Check here: ☐Yes ☐No

20. Would you like information on Exporting? Check here: ☐Yes ☐No

AGREEMENTS AND CERTIFICATIONS

Agreements of non-employment of SBA Personnel: I agree that if SBA approves this loan application I will not, for at least two years, hire as an employee or consultant anyone that was employed by the SBA during the one year period prior to the disbursement of the loan.

Certification: I certify: (a) I have not paid anyone connected with the Federal Government for help in getting this loan. I also agree to report to the SBA office of the Inspector General, Washington, D.C. 20416 any Federal Government employee who offers, in return for any type of compensation, to help get this loan approved.

(b) All information in this application and the Exhibits are true and complete to the best of my knowledge and are submitted to SBA so SBA can decide whether to grant a loan or participate with a lending institution in a loan to me. I agree to pay for or reimburse SBA for the cost of any surveys, title or mortgage examinations, appraisals, credit reports, etc., performed by non-SBA personnel provided I have given my consent.

(c) I understand that I need not pay anybody to deal with SBA. I have read and understand SBA Form 159 which explains SBA policy on representatives and their fees.

(d) As consideration for any Management, Technical, and Business Development Assistance that may be provided, I waive all claims against SBA and its consultants.

If you make a statement that you know to be false or if you over value a security in order to help obtain a loan under the provisions of the Small Business Act, you can be fined up to $5,000 or be put in jail for up to two years, or both.

If Applicant is a proprietor or general partner, sign below.

By: _____
                                                        Date

If Applicant is a Corporation, sign below:

_____
Corporate Name and Seal   Date

By: _____
                        Signature of President

Attested by: _____
                        Signature of Corporate Secretary

APPLICANT'S CERTIFICATION

By my signature I certify that I have read and received a copy of the "STATEMENTS REQUIRED BY LAW AND EXECUTIVE ORDER" which was attached to this application. My signature represents my agreement to comply with the approval of my loan request and to comply, whenever applicable, with the hazard insurance, lead-based paint, civil rights or other limitations in this notice.

Each Proprietor, each General Partner, each Limited Partner or Stockholder owning 20% or more, and each Guarantor must sign. Each person should sign only once.

Business Name _____

_____   By _____
Date   Signature and Title

_____
Date   Signature

_____
Date   Signature

_____
Date   Signature

_____
Date   Signature

U.S. SMALL BUSINESS ADMINISTRATION

SCHEDULE OF COLLATERAL
Exhibit A

OMB Approval No.: 3245-0016
Expiration Date: 10-31-98

Applicant		
Street Address		
City	State	Zip Code

LIST ALL COLLATERAL TO BE USED AS SECURITY FOR THIS LOAN

Section I - REAL ESTATE

Attach a copy of the deed(s) containing a full legal description of the land and show the location (street address) and city where the deed(s) is recorded. Following the address below, give a brief description of the improvements, such as size, type of construction, use, number of stories, and present condition (use additional sheet if more space is required).

LIST PARCELS OF REAL ESTATE

Address	Year Acquired	Original Cost	Market Value	Amount of Lien	Name of Lienholder

Description(s)

SECTION II - PERSONAL PROPERTY

All items listed herein must show manufacturer or make, model, year, and serial number. Items with no serial number must be clearly identified (use additional sheet if more space is required).

Description - Show Manufacturer, Model, Serial No.	Year Acquired	Original Cost	Market Value	Current Lien Balance	Name of Lienholder

All information contained herein is TRUE and CORRECT to the best of my knowldege. I understand that FALSE statements may result in forfeiture of benefits and possible fine and prosecution by the U.S. Attorney General (Ref. 18 U.S.C. 100).

_____   Date _____

_____   Date _____

SBA LOAN NO.

COMPENSATION AGREEMENT FOR SERVICES IN CONNECTION WITH APPLICATION AND LOAN FROM (OR IN PARTICIPATION WITH) SMALL BUSINESS ADMINISTRATION

The undersigned representative (attorney, accountant, engineer, appraiser, etc.) hereby agrees that the undersigned has not and will not, directly or indirectly, charge or receive any payment in connection with the application for or the making of the loan except for services actually performed on behalf of the Applicant. The undersigned further agrees that the amount of payment for such services shall not exceed an amount deemed reasonable by SBA (and, if it is a participation loan, by the participating lending institution), and to refund any amount in excess of that deemed reasonable by SBA (and the participating institution). This agreement shall supersede any other agreement covering payment for such services.

A general description of the services performed, or to be performed, by the undersigned and the compensation paid or to be paid are set forth below. If the total compensation in any case exceeds $1,000 (or $300 for: (1) regular business loans of $15,000 or less; or (2) all disaster home loans) or if SBA should otherwise require, the services must be itemized on a schedule attached showing each date services were performed, time spent each day, and description of service rendered on each day listed.

The undersigned Applicant and representative hereby certify that no other fees have been charged or will be charged by the representative in connection with this loan, unless provided for in the loan authorization specifically approved by SBA.

GENERAL DESCRIPTION OF SERVICES

Paid Previously $ _____
Additional Amount to be Paid $ _____
Total Compensation $ _____

(Section 13 of the Small Business Act (15 USC 642) requires disclosures concerning fees. Parts 103, 108, and 120 of Title 13 of the Code of Federal Regulations contain provisions covering appearances and compensation of persons representing SBA applicants. Section 103.13-5 authorizes the suspension or revocation of the privilege of any such person to appear before SBA for charging a fee deemed unreasonable by SBA for services actually performed, charging of unreasonable expenses, or violation of this agreement. Whoever commits any fraud, by false or misleading statement or representation, or by conspiracy, shall be subject to the penalty of any applicable Federal or State statute.)

Dated _____ , 19 _____

_____
(Representative)

By _____

The Applicant hereby certifies to SBA that the above representations, description of services and amounts are correct and satisfactory to the Applicant

Dated _____ , 19 _____

_____
(Applicant)

By _____

The participating lending institution hereby certifies that the above representations of service rendered and amounts charged are reasonable and satisfactory to it.

Dated _____ , 19 _____

_____
(Lender)

By _____

NOTE: Foregoing certification must be executed, if by a corporation, in corporate name by duly authorized officer and duly attested; if by a partnership, in the firm name, together with signature of a general partner.

PLEASE NOTE: The estimated burden hours for the completion of this form of SBA Form 147, 148, 159, 160, 160A, 529B, 928, and 1059 is 6 hours per response. You will not be required to respond to this information collection if a valid OMB approval number is not displayed. If you have any questions or comments concerning this estimate or other aspects of this information collection, please contact the U.S. Small Business Administration, Chief, Administrative Information Branch, Washington D.C. 20416 and/or Office of Management and Budget, Clearance Officer, Paperwork Reduction Project (3245-0201), Washington, D.C. 20503.

This form was electronically produced by Elite Federal Forms, Inc.

SBA FORM 159 (2-93) REF SOP 70 50 Use 7-89 edition until exhausted Pg 107

Federal Recycling Program Printed on Recycled Paper

U.S. SMALL BUSINESS ADMINISTRATION
POLICY AND REGULATIONS CONCERNING REPRESENTATIVES AND THEIR FEES

An applicant for a loan from SBA may obtain the assistance of any attorney, accountant, engineer, appraiser or oth representative to aid him in the preparation and presentation of his application to SBA; however, such representation is r mandatory. In the event a loan is approved, the services of an attorney may be necessary to assist in the preparation closing documents, title abstracts, etc. SBA will allow the payment of reasonable fees or other compensation for servic performed by such representatives on behalf of the applicant.

There are no "authorized representatives" of SBA, other than our regular salaried employees. Payment of any fee gratuity to SBA employees is illegal and will subject the parties to such a transaction to prosecution.

SBA Regulations (Part 103, Sec. 103.13-5(c)) prohibit representatives from charging or proposing to charge any continge fee for any services performed in connection with an SBA loan unless the amount of such fee bears a necessary a reasonable relationship to the services actually performed; or to charge for any expenses which are not deemed by SBA have been necessary in connection with the application. The Regulations (Part 120, Sec. 120.104-2) also prohibit the payme of any bonus, brokerage fee or commission in connection with SBA loans.

In line with these Regulations SBA will not approve placement or finder's fees for the use or attempted use of influence obtaining or trying to obtain an SBA loan, or fees based solely upon a percentage of the approved loan or any part thereof.

Fees which will be approved will be limited to reasonable sums of services actually rendered in connection with t application or the closing, based upon the time and effort required, the qualifications of the representative and the nature a extent of the services rendered by such representatives. Representatives of loan applicants will be required to execute agreement as to their compensation for services rendered in connection with said loan.

It is the responsibility of the applicant to set forth in the appropriate section of the application the names of all persons firms engaged by or on behalf of the applicant. Applicants are required to advise the Regional Office in writing the names a fees of any representatives engaged by the applicant subsequent to the filing of the application. This reporting requirement approved under OMB Approval Number 3245-0016.

Any loan applicant having any question concerning the payments of fees, or the reasonableness of fees, shou communicate with the Field Office where the application is filed.

PERSONAL FINANCIAL STATEMENT

U.S. SMALL BUSINESS ADMINISTRATION

As of _____ , _____

Complete this form for: (1) each proprietor, or (2) each limited partner who owns 20% or more interest and each general partner, or (3) each stockholder owning 20% or more of voting stock, or (4) any person or entity providing a guaranty on the loan.

Name	Business Phone
Residence Address	Residence Phone
City, State, & Zip Code	
Business Name of Applicant/Borrower	

ASSETS	(Omit Cents)	LIABILITIES	(Omit Cents)
Cash on hands & in Banks	$ _____	Accounts Payable	$ _____
Savings Accounts	$ _____	Notes Payable to Banks and Others	$ _____
IRA or Other Retirement Account	$ _____	(Describe in Section 2)	
Accounts & Notes Receivable	$ _____	Installment Account (Auto)	$ _____
Life Insurance-Cash Surrender Value Only . . .	$ _____	Mo. Payments $ _____	
(Complete Section 8)		Installment Account (Other)	$ _____
Stocks and Bonds	$ _____	Mo. Payments $ _____	
(Describe in Section 3)		Loan on Life Insurance	$ _____
Real Estate	$ _____	Mortgages on Real Estate	$ _____
(Describe in Section 4)		(Describe in Section 4)	
Automobile-Present Value	$ _____	Unpaid Taxes	$ _____
Other Personal Property	$ _____	(Describe in Section 6)	
(Describe in Section 5)		Other Liabilities	$ _____
Other Assets	$ _____	(Describe in Section 7)	
(Describe in Section 5)		Total Liabilities -	$ _____
		Net Worth	$ _____
Total	$ _____	**Total**	$ _____

Section 1. Source of Income		Contingent Liabilities	
Salary	$ _____	As Endorser or Co-Maker	$ _____
Net Investment Income	$ _____	Legal Claims & Judgments	$ _____
Real Estate Income	$ _____	Provision for Federal Income Tax	$ _____
Other Income (Describe below)*	$ _____	Other Special Debt	$ _____

Description of Other Income in Section 1.

Alimony or child support payments need not be disclosed in "Other Income" unless it is desired to have such payments counted toward total income.

(Use attachments if necessary. Each attachment must be identified as a part of this statement and signed.)

Name and Address of Noteholder(s)	Original Balance	Current Balance	Payment Amount	Frequency (monthly, etc.)	How Secured or Endorsed Type of Collateral

SBA Form 413 (2-94) Use 5-91 Edition until stock is exhausted. Ref: SOP 50-10 and 50-30

Page 109

This form was electronically produced by Elite Federal Forms, Inc.

Section 3.

Number of Shares	Name of Securities	Cost	Market Value Quotation/Exchange	Date of Quotation/Exchange	Total Value

Section 4.

(List each parcel separately. Use attachment if necessary. Each attachment must be identified as a part of this statement and signed.)

	Property A	Property B	Property C
Type of Property			
Address			
Date Purchased			
Original Cost			
Present Market Value			
Name & Address of Mortgage Holder			
Mortgage Account Number			
Mortgage Balance			
Amount of Payment per Month/Year			
Status of Mortgage			

Section 5.

(Describe, and if any is pledged as security, state name and address of lien holder, amount of lien, terms of payment and if delinquent, describe delinquency)

Section 6. Unpaid Taxes.

(Describe in detail, as to type, to whom payable, when due, amount, and to what property, if any, a tax lien attaches.)

Section 7. Other Liabilities.

(Describe in detail.)

Section 8. Life Insurance Held.

(Give face amount and cash surrender value of policies - name of insurance company and beneficiaries)

I authorize SBA/Lender to make inquiries as necessary to verify the accuracy of the statements made and to determine my creditworthiness. I certify the above and the statements contained in the attachments are true and accurate as of the stated date(s). These statements are made for the purpose of either obtaining a loan or guaranteeing a loan. I understand FALSE statements may result in forfeiture of benefits and possible prosecution by the U.S. Attorney General (Reference 18 U.S.C. 1001).

Signature:	Date:	Social Security Number:
Signature:	Date:	Social Security Number:

PLEASE NOTE: The estimated average burden hours for the completion of this form is 1.5 hours per response. If you have questions or comments concerning this estimate or any other aspect of this information, please contact Chief, Administrative Branch, U.S. Small Business Administration, Washington, D.C. 20416, and Clearance Officer, Paper Reduction Project (3245-0188), Office of Management and Budget, Washington, D.C. 20503.

Case Number: _____

U.S. Small Business Administration
Request for Counseling

Your Name (First, Middle, Last)	2. Telephone Number(s)
	Home _____
	Business _____
Email address	Fax _____

Street Address	5. City	6. County	7. State	8. Zip

Race (mark one or more)	10. Ethnicity	12. Within the last two years, have you ever received:	13. Veteran Status
Native American or Alaskan Native ☐	a. Hispanic Origin ☐ b. Not of Hispanic Origin ☐	a. Aid to Families with Dependent Children (AFDC)	a. Veteran ☐ b. Disabled Veteran ☐ c. Vietnam Era Veteran ☐ d. Non-Veteran ☐
Asian ☐	11. Business Owner Gender	Yes ☐ No ☐	
Black or African American ☐	a. Male ☐	b. Temporary Assistance to Needy Families (TANF)	
Native Hawaiian or other Pacific Islander ☐	b. Female ☐		
White ☐	c. Male/Female ☐	Yes ☐ No ☐	

How did you hear of us?

Word of Mouth ☐	d. Chamber of Commerce ☐	g. Television ☐	j. SBA ☐
Bank ☐	e. Internet ☐	h. Magazine ☐	
Newspapers ☐	f. Radio ☐	i. Other _____	

Describe the nature of the counseling you are seeking.

Currently in Business? Yes ☐ No ☐ (If no, skip to line 20)   Is this a Home-based Business? Yes ☐ No ☐

Type of Business

Name of Company:	19. How long in business?

Indicate preferred date & time for appointment:

Date: _____   Time: _____

request business management counseling service from a Small Business Administration Resource Partner. I agree to cooperate should I be selected to participate in surveys designed to evaluate SBA assistance services. I authorize SBA to furnish relevant information to the assigned management counselor(s). I understand that any information disclosed to be held in strict confidence by him/her.

further understand that any counselor has agreed not to: (1) recommend goods or services from sources in which he/she has an interest and (2) accept fees or commissions developing from this counseling relationship. In consideration of the counselor(s) furnishing management or technical assistance, I waive all claims against SBA personnel, SCORE and its host organizations, and other SBA Resource Counselors arising from this assistance.

ase note: The estimated burden for completing this form is 15 minutes per response. You will not be required to respond to this information collection if a d OMB approval number is not displayed. If you have questions or comments concerning this estimate or other aspects of this information, please contact U.S. Small Business Administration, Chief, Administrative Information Branch, Washington, DC 20416 and/or Office of Management and Budget, arance Officer, Paperwork Reduction Project (3245-0091), Washington, DC 20503.

gnature: _____   Date: _____

Chapter Number _____

Branch Name _____

OMB Approval No. 3245-0(
Expiration Date: 06/30/01

Telephone Counseling ☐

E-mail Counseling ☐

Case Number _____

Date Entered _____

Entry by _____

U.S. Small Business Administration

Counseling Information Sheet

1. Client Information:	2. Appointment Scheduled:
Name: _____ First Middle Last	With (counselor) _____ On (date) _____ (time) _____ AM / P

3. a) New case ☐   b) Follow-on ☐   c) Close out ☐   Conf. By _____ on _____

4. Legal Entity: ☐ Sole Proprietorship ☐ Partnership ☐ Corporation ☐ S-Corporation ☐ LLC

5. Client objective / Counseling purpose: _____

_____

_____

6. Primary area(s) of counseling:

a.	Start-ups ☐	d.	Financial ☐	g.	Intl. Trade ☐	j.	Franchises ☐
b.	Capital Sources ☐	e.	Human Resources ☐	h.	Business Plan ☐	k.	Other _____
c.	Marketing/Sales ☐	f.	Technology ☐	i.	Buy/Dell ☐	l.	Other _____

7. Counselor's Notes:

8. Counselor Name(s) _____ 9. Counseling Date _____ 10. Counseling Hours _____	11. SBA Client: a) Borrower ☐ d) COC ☐ b) Applicant ☐ e) Surety Bond ☐ c) 8(a) Client ☐

12. Has client been informed about other SBA resources? ☐ yes ☐ no

OMB APPROVAL NO.3245-0178
Expiration Date:7/31/2000

United States of America
SMALL BUSINESS ADMINISTRATION
STATEMENT OF PERSONAL HISTORY

Please Read Carefully - Print or Type

Each member of the small business concern or the development company requesting assistance must submit this form in TRIPLICATE for filing with the SBA application. This form must be filled out and submitted by:

1. If a sole proprietorship by the proprietor.
2. If a partnership by each partner.
3. If a corporation or a development company, by each officer, director, and additionally by each holder of 20% or more of the voting stock.
4. Any other person including a hired manager, who has authority to speak for and commit the borrower in the management of the business.

ne and Address of Applicant (Firm Name)(Street, City, State, and ZIP Code)	SBA District/Disaster Area Office
	Amount Applied for (when applicable) File No. (if known)
Personal Statement of: (State name in full, if no middle name, state (NMN), or if initial only, indicate initial.) List all former names used, and dates each name was used. Use separate sheet if necessary.	Name and Address of participating lender or surety co. (when applicable and known)
First Middle Last	2. Date of Birth (Month, day, and year)
	3. Place of Birth: (City & State or Foreign Country)
Give the percentage of ownership or stock owned or to be owned in the small business concern or the Development Company Social Security No.	U.S. Citizen? ☐ YES ☐ NO If no, give alien registration number: _____

Present residence address:
From:
To:
Address:

Most recent prior address (omit if over 10 years ago):
From:
To:
Address:

Home Telephone No. (Include A/C):

Business Telephone No. (Include A/C):

S AGAINST SBA'S POLICY TO PROVIDE ASSISTANCE TO PERSONS NOT OF GOOD CHARACTER; THEREFORE, CONSIDERATION IS GIVEN TO A RSON'S BEHAVIOR, INTEGRITY, CANDOR, AND DISPOSITION TOWARD CRIMINAL ACTIONS. IT IS ALSO AGAINST SBA'S POLICY TO PROVIDE SISTANCE NOT IN THE BEST INTEREST OF THE UNITED STATES; FOR EXAMPLE, IF THERE IS REASON TO BELIEVE THE EFFECT OF SUCH SISTANCE WILL BE TO ENCOURAGE OR SUPPORT, DIRECTLY OR INDIRECTLY, ACTIVITIES HARMFUL TO THE SECURITY OF THE UNITED ATES.

EREFORE, IT IS IMPORTANT THAT THE NEXT THREE QUESTIONS BE ANSWERED TRUTHFULLY AND COMPLETELY. AN ARREST OR NVICTION RECORD WILL NOT NECESSARILY DISQUALIFY YOU; HOWEVER, AN UNTRUTHFUL ANSWER WILL CAUSE YOUR APPLICATION TO BE NIED.

YOU ANSWER "YES" TO 6, 7, OR 8, FURNISH DETAILS IN A SEPARATE EXHIBIT. INCLUDE DATES, LOCATION, FINES, SENTENCES, WHETHER SDEMEANOR OR FELONY, DATES OF PAROLE/PROBATION, UNPAID FINES OR PENALTIES, NAME(S) UNDER WHICH CHARGED, AND ANY OTHER RTINENT INFORMATION.

Are you presently under indictment, on parole or probation?
☐ Yes ☐ No   (If yes, indicate date parole or probation is to expire.)

Have you ever been charged with and or arrested for any criminal offense other than a minor motor vehicle violation? Include offenses which have been dismissed, discharged, or not prosecuted (All arrests and charges must be disclosed and explained on an attached sheet.)
☐ Yes ☐ No

Have you ever been convicted, placed on pretrial diversion, or placed on any form of probation, including adjudication withheld pending probation, for any criminal offense other than a minor vehicle violation?
☐ Yes ☐ No

authorize the Small Business Administration Office of Inspector General to request criminal record information about me from criminal justice agencies for the purpose of etermining my eligibility for programs authorized by the Small Business Act, as amended.

UTION: Knowingly making a false statement on this form is a violation of Federal law and could result in criminal prosecution, significant civil penalties, and a denial of your loan, ty bond, or other program participation. A false statement is punishable under 18 USC 1001 by imprisonment of not more than five years and/or a fine of not more than $10,000; er 15 USC 645 by imprisonment of not more than two years and/or a fine of not more than $5,000; and, if submitted to a Federally insured institution, under 18 USC 1014 by risonment of not more than twenty years and/or a fine of not more than $1,000,000.

nature	Title	Date

ency Use Only

☐ Fingerprints Waived   Date   Approving Authority

☐ Fingerprints Required

Date Sent to OIG   Date   Approving Authority

11. ☐ Cleared for Processing   Date   Approving Authority

☐ Request a Character Evaluation   Date   Approving Authority

se Note: The estimated burden for completing this form is 15 minutes per response. You will not be required to respond to this information if a valid OMB approval number ot displayed. If you have questions or comments concerning this estimate or other aspects of this information collection, please contact the U.S. Small Business inistration, Chief, Administrative Information Branch, Washington, D.C. 20416 and/or Office of Management and Budget, Clearance Officer, Paperwork Reduction Project.

A 912 (5-97) SOP 5010.4 Previous Edition Obsolete   This form was electronically produced by Elite Federal Forms, Inc.

Certification Regarding
Debarment, Suspension, Ineligibility and Voluntary Exclusion
Lower Tier Covered Transactions

This certification is required by the regulations implementing Executive Order 12549, Debarment and Suspension, 13 CFR Part 145. The regulations were published as Part VII of the May 26, 1988 *Federal Register* (pages 19160-19211). Copies of the regulations may be obtained by contacting the person to which this proposal is submitted.

(BEFORE COMPLETING CERTIFICATION, READ INSTRUCTIONS ON REVERSE)

(1) The prospective lower tier participant certifies, by submission of this proposal, that neither it nor its principals are presently debarred, suspended, proposed for disbarment, declared ineligible, or voluntarily excluded from participation in this transaction by any Federal department or agency.

(2) Where the prospective lower tier participant is unable to certify to any of the statements in this certification, such prospective participant shall attach an explanation to this proposal.

Business Name _____

Date _____   By _____
                                                     Name and Title of Authorized Representative

                                                     _____
                                                     Signature of Authorized Representative

Federal Recycling Program   Printed on Recycled Paper

INSTRUCTIONS FOR CERTIFICATION

1. By signing and submitting this proposal, the prospective lower tier participant is providing the certification set out below.

2. The certification in this clause is a material representation of fact upon which reliance was placed when this transaction was entered into. If it is later determined that the prospective lower tier participant knowingly rendered an erroneous certification, in addition to other remedies available to the Federal Government, the department or agency with which this transaction originated may pursue available remedies, including suspension and/or debarment.

3. The prospective lower tier participant shall provide immediate written notice to the person to which this proposal is submitted if at any time the prospective lower tier participant learns that its certification was erroneous when submitted or has become erroneous by reason of changed circumstances.

4. The terms "covered transaction," "debarred," "suspended," "ineligible," "lower tier covered transaction," "participant," "person," "primary covered transaction," "principal," "proposal," and "voluntarily excluded," as used in this clause, have the meanings set out in the Definitions and Coverage sections of the rules implementing Executive Order 12549. You may contact the person to which this proposal is submitted for assistance in obtaining a copy of those regulations (13CFR Part 145).

5. The prospective lower tier participant agrees by submitting this proposal that, should the proposed covered transaction be entered into, it shall not knowingly enter into any lower tier covered transaction with a person who is debarred, suspended, declared ineligible, or voluntarily excluded from participation in this covered transaction, unless authorized by the department or agency with which this transaction originated.

6. The prospective lower tier participant further agrees by submitting this proposal that it will include the clause titled "Certification Regarding Debarment, Suspension, Ineligibility and Voluntary Exclusion--Lower Tier Covered Transactions," without modification, in all lower tier covered transactions and in all solicitations for lower tier covered transactions.

7. A participant in a covered transaction may rely upon a certification of a prospective participant in a lower tier covered transaction that it is not debarred, suspended, ineligible, or voluntarily excluded from the covered transaction, unless it knows that the certification is erroneous. A participant may decide the method and frequency by which it determines the eligibility of its principals. Each participant may, but is not required to, check the Nonprocurement List.

8. Nothing contained in the foregoing shall be construed to require establishment of a system of records in order to render in good faith the certification required by this clause. The knowledge and information of a participant is not required to exceed that which is normally possessed by a prudent person in the ordinary course of business dealings.

9. Except for transactions authorized under paragraph 5 of these instructions, if a participant in a covered transaction knowingly enters into a lower tier covered transaction with a person who is suspended, debarred, ineligible, or voluntarily excluded from participation in this transaction, in addition to other remedies available to the Federal Government, the department or agency with which this transaction originated may pursue available remedies, including suspension and/or debarment.

STATEMENT REGARDING LOBBYING

Statement for Loan Guarantees and Loan Insurance

The undersigned states, to the best of his or her knowledge and belief, that:

(1)   If any funds have been paid or will be paid to any person for influencing or attempting to influence an officer or employee of any agency, a Member of Congress, an officer or employee of Congress, or an employee of a Member of Congress in connection with this commitment providing for the United States to insure or guarantee a loan, the undersigned shall complete and submit Standard Form LLL, "Disclosure of Lobbying Activities," in accordance with its instructions.

(2)   Submission of this statement is a prerequisite for making or entering into this transaction imposed by Section 1352, Title 31, U.S. Code. Any person who fails to file the required statement shall be subject to a civil penalty of not less than $10,000 and not more than $100,000 for each such failure.

Signature: _____

Date: _____

Name and Title: _____

Federal Recycling Program   Printed on Recycled Paper

SBA Form 1846 (8-92)

SBA
U.S. Small Business Administration

Form **4506**

(Rev. May 1997)

Department of the Treasury
Internal Revenue Service

Request for Copy or Transcript of Tax Form

▸ **Read instructions before completing this form.**

▸ **Type or print clearly. Request may be rejected if the form is incomplete or illegible.**

OMB No. 1545-0429

Note: *Do not use this form to get tax account information. Instead, see instructions below.*

1a	Name shown on tax form. If a joint return, enter the name shown first.	**1b**	First social security number on tax form or employer identification number (See instructions.)
2a	If a joint return, spouse's name shown on tax form	**2b**	Second social security number on tax form

3 Current name, address (including apt., room, or suite no.), city, state, and ZIP code

4 Address, (including apt., room, or suite no.), city, state, and ZIP code shown on the last return filed if different from line 3.

5 If copy of form or a tax return transcript is to be mailed to someone else, enter the third party's name and address.

6 If we cannot find a record of your tax form and you want the payment refunded to the third party, check here . . . . ▸ ☐

7 If name in third party's records differs from line 1a above, enter that name here (see instructions) ▸

8 Check only one box to show what you want. There is **no charge** for items 8a, b, and c.

  a ☐ Tax return transcript of Form 1040 series filed during the **current calendar year** and the **3 prior calendar years**. (see instructions).

  b ☐ Verification of nonfiling.

  c ☐ Form(s) W-2 information (see instructions).

  d ☐ Copy of tax form and all attachments (including Form(s) W-2, schedules, or other forms). **The charge is $23 for each period requested.**

    Note: *If these copies must be certified for court or administrative proceedings, see instructions and check here* . . . . ▸ ☐

9 If this request is to meet a requirement of one of the following, check all boxes that apply.

  ☐ Small Business Administration   ☐ Department of Education   ☐ Department of Veterans Affairs   ☐ Financial institution

10 Tax form number (Form 1040, 1040A, 941, etc.)	**12** Complete only if line 8d is checked. Amount due:
	a Cost for each period . . . .
11 Tax period(s) (year or period ended date). If more than four, see instructions.	**b** Number of tax periods requested on line 11
	c Total cost. Multiply line 12a by line 12b . . . . $
	Full payment must accompany your request. Make check or money order payable to "Internal Revenue Service."

Does not apply to SBA transcript requests

Caution: *Before signing, make sure all items are complete and the form is dated.*

I declare that I am either the taxpayer whose name is shown on line 1a or 2a, or a person authorized to obtain the tax information requested. I am aware that based upon this form, the IRS will release the tax information requested to any party shown on line 5. The IRS has no control over what that party does with the information.

Please Sign Here

Signature. See instructions. If other than taxpayer, attach authorization document.	Date	Telephone number of requester
Title (if line 1a above is a corporation, partnership, estate, or trust)		Best time to call
Spouse's signature	Date	**TRY A TAX RETURN TRANSCRIPT** (see line 8a instructions)

Instructions

Section references are to the Internal Revenue Code.

TIP: If you had your tax form filled in by a paid preparer, check first to see if you can get a copy from the preparer. This may save you both time and money.

Purpose of Form.—Use Form 4506 to get a tax return transcript, verification that you did not file a Federal return, Form W-2, information, or a copy of a tax form. Allow 6 weeks after you file a tax form before you request a copy of it or a transcript. For W-2 information, wait 13 months after the end of the year in which the wages were earned. For example, wait until Feb. 1999 to request W-2 information for wages earned in 1997.

Do not use this form to request Forms 1099 or tax account information. See this page for details on how to get these items.

Note: *Form 4506 must be received by the IRS within 60 calendar days after the date you signed and dated the request.*

How Long Will It Take?—You can get a tax return transcript or verification of nonfiling within 7 to 10 workdays after the IRS receives your request. It can take up to 60 calendar days to get a copy of a tax form or W-2 information. To avoid any delay, be sure to furnish all the information asked for on Form 4506.

Forms 1099.—If you need a copy of a Form 1099, contact the payer. If the payer cannot help you, call or visit the IRS to get Form 1099 information.

Tax Account Information.—If you need a statement of your tax account showing any later changes that you or the IRS made to the original return, request tax account information. Tax account information lists

(Continued on back)

For Privacy Act and Paperwork Reduction Act Notice, see back of form.

Cat. No. 41721E

Form **4506** (Rev. 5-97)

This form was electronically produced by Elite Federal Forms, Inc.

certain items from you return, including any later changes.

To request tax account information, write or visit an IRS office or call the IRS at the number listed in your telephone directory.

If you want your tax account information sent to a third party, complete **Form 8821**, Tax Information Authorization. You may get this form by phone (call 1-800-829-3676) or on the Internet (at http://www.irs.ustreas.gov).

Line 1b.—Enter your employer identification number (EIN) only if you are requesting a copy of a **business** tax form. Otherwise, enter the first social security number (SSN) shown on the tax form.

Line 2b.—If requesting a copy or transcript of a joint tax form, enter the second SSN shown on the tax form.

Note: *If you do not complete line 1b and, if applicable, line 2b, there may be a delay in processing your request.*

Line 5.—If you want someone else to receive the tax form or tax return transcript (such as a CPA, an enrolled agent, a scholarship board, or a mortgage lender), enter the name and address of the individual. If we cannot find a record of your tax form, we will notify the third party directly that we cannot fill the request.

Line 7.—Enter the name of the client, student, or applicant if it is different from the name shown on line 1a. For example, the name on line 1a may be the parent of a student applying for financial aid. In this case, you would enter the student's name on line 7 so the scholarship board can associate the tax form or tax return transcript with their file.

Line 8a.—If want a tax return transcript, check this box. Also, on line 10 enter the tax form number and on line 11 enter the tax period, for which you want the transcript.

A tax return transcript is available for any returns of the 1040 series (Form 1040, Form 1040A, 1040EZ, etc.). It shows most line items from the original return, including accompanying forms and schedules. In many cases, a transcript will meet the requirement of any lending institution such as a financial institution, the Department of Education, or the Small Business Administration. It may also be used to verify that you did not claim any itemized deductions for a residence.

Note: *A tax return transcript does not reflect any changes you or the IRS made to the original return. If you want a statement of your tax account with the changes, see Tax Account Information on page 1.*

Line 8b.—Check this box only if you want proof from the IRS that you did not file a return for the year. Also, on line 11 enter the tax period for which you want verification of nonfiling.

Line 8c.—If you want only Form(s) W-2 information, check this box. Also, on line 10 enter "Forms(s) W-2 only" and on line 11 enter the tax period for which you want the information.

You may receive a copy of your actual Form W-2 or a transcript of the information, depending on how your employer filed the form. However, state withholding information is not shown on a transcript. If you have filed your tax return for the year the wages were earned, you can get a copy of the actual Form W-2 by requesting a complete copy of your return and paying the required fee.

Contact your employer if you have lost your current year's Form W-2 or have not received it by the time you are ready to prepare your tax return.

Note: *If you are requesting information about your spouse's Form W-2, your spouse must sign Form 4506.*

Line 8d.—If you want a certified copy of a tax form for court or administrative proceedings, check the box to the right of line 8d. It will take at least 60 days to process your request.

Line 11.—Enter the year(s) of the tax form or tax return transcript you want. For fiscal-year filers or requests for quarterly tax forms, enter the date the period ended; for example, 3/31/96, 6/30/96, etc. If you need more than four different tax periods, use additional Forms 4506. Tax forms filed 6 or more years ago may not be available for making copies. However, tax account information is generally still available for these periods.

Line 12c.—Write your SSN or EIN and "Form 4506 Request" on your check or money order. If we cannot fill your request, we will refund your payment.

Signature.—Requests for copies of tax forms or tax return transcripts to be sent to a third party must be signed by the person whose name is shown on line 1a or by a person authorized to receive the requested information.

Copies of tax forms or tax return transcripts for a jointly filed return may be furnished to either the husband or the wife. Only one signature is required. However, see the line 8c instructions. Sign Form 4506 exactly as your name appeared on the original tax form. If you changed your name, **also** sign your current name.

For a corporation, the signature of the president of the corporation, or any principal officer and the secretary, or the principal officer and another officer are generally required. For more details on who may obtain tax information on corporations, partnerships, estates, and trusts, see section 6103.

If you are not the taxpayer shown on line 1a, you must attach your authorization to receive a copy of the requested tax form or tax return transcript. You may **attach a copy of the authorization document** if the original has already been filed with the IRS. This will generally be a **power of attorney** (Form 2848), or **other authorization,** such as Form 8821, or evidence of entitlement (for Title 11 Bankruptcy or Receivership Proceedings). If the taxpayer is deceased, you must send Letters Testamentary or other evidence to establish that you are authorized to act for the taxpayer's estate.

Where To File.—Mail Form 4506 with the correct total payment attached, if required, to the **Internal Revenue Service Center** for the place where you lived when the requested tax form was filed.

Note: *You must use a separate form for each service center from which you are requesting a copy of your tax form or tax return transcript.*

If you lived in:	Use this address:
New Jersey, New York (New York City and counties of Nassau, Rockland, Suffolk, and Westchester)	1040 Waverly Ave. Photocopy Unit Stop 532 Holtsville, NY 11742
New York (all other counties), Connecticut, Maine, Massachusetts, New Hampshire, Rhode Island, Vermont	310 Lowell St. Photocopy Unit Stop 679 Andover, MA 01810
Florida, Georgia, South Carolina	4800 Buford Hwy. Photocopy Unit Stop 91 Doraville, GA 30362
Indiana, Kentucky, Michigan, Ohio, West Virginia	P.O. Box 145500 Photocopy Unit Stop 524 Cincinnati, OH 45250
Kansas, New Mexico, Oklahoma, Texas	3651 South Interregional Hwy. Photocopy Unit Stop 6716 Austin, TX 73301
Alaska, Arizona, California (counties of Alpine, Amador, Butte, Calaveras, Colusa, Contra Costa, Del Norte, El Dorado, Glenn, Humboldt, Lake, Lassen, Marin, Mendocino, Modoc, Napa, Nevada, Placer, Plumas, Sacramento, San Joaquin Shasta, Sierra, Siskiyou, Solano, Sonoma, Sutter, Tehama, Trinity, Yolo, and Yuba), Colorado, Idaho, Montana, Nebraska, Nevada, North Dakota, Oregon, South Dakota, Utah, Washington, Wyoming	P.O. Box 9941 Photocopy Unit Stop 6734 Ogden, UT 84409
California (all other counties), Hawaii	5045 E. Butler Avenue Photocopy Unit Stop 52180 Fresno, CA 93888
Illinois, Iowa, Minnesota, Missouri, Wisconsin	2306 E. Bannister Road Photocopy Unit Stop 57A Kansas City, MO 64999
Alabama, Arkansas, Louisiana, Mississippi, North Carolina, Tennessee	P.O. Box 30309 Photocopy Unit Stop 46 Memphis, TN 38130
Delaware, District of Columbia, Maryland, Pennsylvania, Virginia, a foreign country, or A.P.O. or F.P.O address	11601 Roosevelt Blvd. Photocopy Unit DP 536 Philadelphia, PA 19255

Privacy Act and Paperwork Reduction Act Notice.—We ask for the information on this form to establish your right to gain access to your tax form or transcript under the Internal Revenue Code, including sections 6103 and 6109. We need it to gain access to your tax form or transcript in our files and properly respond to your request. If you do not furnish the information, we will not be able to fill your request. We may give the information to the Department of Justice or other appropriate law enforcement official, as provided by law.

You are not required to provide the information requested on a form that is subject to the Paperwork Reduction Act unless the form displays a valid OMB control number. Books or records relating to a form or its instructions must be retained as long as their contents may become material in the administration of any Internal Revenue law. Generally, tax returns and return information are confidential, as required by section 6103.

The time needed to complete and file this form will vary depending on individual circumstances. The estimated average time is: **Recordkeeping,** 13 min.; **Learning about the law or the form,** 7 min.; **Preparing the form,** 26 min.; and **Copying, assembling, and sending the form to the IRS,** 17 min.

If you have comments concerning the accuracy of these time estimates or suggestions for making this form simpler, we would be happy to hear from you. You can write to the Tax Forms Committee, Western Area Distribution Center, Rancho Cordova, CA 95743-0001. DO NOT send the form to this address. Instead, see **Where To File** on this page.

Glossary of useful terms

7(a)-A

7(a) Guaranteed Loan Program

A Small Business Administration program providing funds that are reasonably affordable to small firms located in areas having either high unemployment or large numbers of low-income residents.

7(a) Loan Guaranty

The 7(a) Loan Guaranty Program is one of SBA's primary lending programs. It provides loans to small businesses unable to secure financing on reasonable terms through normal lending channels. The program operates through private-sector lenders that provide loans which are, in turn, guaranteed by the SBA-the Agency has no funds for direct lending or grants.

8(a) Participant Loan Program

A Small Business Administration program making financial assistance available to 8(a)-certified firms and minority advocacy groups.

Accounts Payable

The money owed to your suppliers.

Accounts Receivable

The money owed to you by your customers or clients.

Active Corps of Executives (ACE)

A Small Business Administration sponsored program, staffed by volunteers active in business, who offer consulting assistance to small businesses.

Asset

Any resources or rights having commercial or exchange value that are owned by a business, institution, or individual, including those having probable future benefit and the ability to contribute to future income.

B-Ca

Balance Sheet

An itemized statement of your business' financial position at any given point in time. Your balance sheet should show that your total assets equal your total liabilities, plus your equity.

Break-even Point

The number of units you need to sell, at a specific price, to cover the fixed and variable costs. Profit results when a larger number of units are sold.

Business Development Corporations (BDC)

Privately-owned business development companies chartered by states that make loans available to small businesses.

Business Development Program

An extensive and diversified Small Business Administration program offering free conferences, counseling, courses, problem clinics, publications, and workshops oriented toward improving the management skills of small business owners.

Business Information Centers (BIC)

Centers established by the Small Business Administration providing free access to hardware, software, books, publications, and counseling services for entrepreneurs.

Business Overhead Expenses

Your cost of rent, taxes, utilities, interior decoration, and any other business operating expenses, excluding labor and materials.

Business Plan

Usually a written document detailing a new or ongoing business strategy, sales projection, and key personnel; and providing a strategic foundation for growth. These plans are often used to obtain financing.

Capital Assets

Any tangible or intangible assets that are held for long-term investment.

Capital Budget

Your itemized list of planned investment expenditures and a schedule showing the timing associated with each expenditure.

Capital Expense

An outlay of money to acquire or improve capital assets (e.g., buildings, equipment, or machinery).

Ca-Co

Cash-flow Statement

A summary of your cash transactions for a period of time used for budgeting and managing internal financial planning and control.

Certificate of Competency (COC)

A certificate issued by the Small Business Administration certifying a small company's competency to perform a specific government contract.

Certificate of Deposit

A bank statement certifying that the named individual has a particular sum on deposit.

Certified Development Company (504 Loan) Program

This program, commonly referred to as the 504 program, makes long term loans available for purchasing land, buildings, and machinery and equipment, and for building, modernizing or renovating existing facilities and sites.

Certified Development Company (504) Loans

A loan program linking the Small Business Administration, a certified development company, and a private lender in long-term financing packages and providing assistance for projects costing over $1 million.

Certified Development Company Program

A private, public sector non-profit corporation that's set up to contribute to the economic development of a community or region.

Certified Lenders Program

A Small Business Administration program for expediting loan processing where banks, acting under Small Business Administration supervision, manage much of the paperwork and review client financial status. The banks thereby relieve the Small Business Administration personnel to address other small business issues.

Certified Public Accountant (CPA)

An accountant who has met the state's education, experience, and ethical requirements for certification as a licensed public accountant.

Collateral

Assets that you provide to the lender as security for a loan.

Controller

The individual within your organization who is responsible for the firm's accounting, auditing, and budgeting.

Co-Di

Corporation

A legally recognized, organizational structure representing an autonomous entity characterized by transferable ownership.

Cost of Goods Sold or Cost of Sales

Those costs you incur to either produce or acquire the units that are sold. The cost is determined by comparing the beginning inventory, plus purchases, minus the ending inventory.

Current Asset

An asset usually converted to cash within one year, or within the firm's normal operating cycle.

Current Liability

A liability usually paid within one year, or within the firm's normal operating cycle.

Debt

Money, goods, or services owed by one party to another to be paid in accordance with either an implied or written agreement, including bonds, notes, or other forms of paper indicating amounts owed and payable.

Department of Energy Loan

Loans and guarantees for firms engaged in developing, manufacturing, retailing, or servicing of specific energy measures.

Department of Housing and Urban Development Loans

Grant and loan programs for construction of commercial and residential buildings to rehabilitate needy areas in targeted cities.

Department of Interior Grants

An historic preservation-grants program used for the restoration of run-down properties that have been declared historic sites by a state agency.

Depreciation, Accelerated

Depreciation methods that allow larger depreciation deductions during the early years of a project.

Depreciation

The reduction in the book value of an asset, usually deducted from taxable income.

Disabled Veterans Loans

Loans for disabled and Vietnam-era veterans to start, operate, or expand a small business.

Di-Fa

Dividend

Distribution of corporate earnings to shareholders as decided by the board of directors and usually paid quarterly.

Dome Ledgers

Forms standardized for bookkeeping and providing an established system for recording your transactions.

Double Taxation

Taxation of both corporate income and personal income when income is distributed to shareholders as dividends.

EBIT

Earnings before income and taxes.

Economic Development Administration Loan

A U.S. Department of Commerce agency that makes loans and guarantees available to new and existing businesses in depressed areas.

Economic Injury Disaster Loan

Loans to small businesses that have suffered substantial economic loss resulting from disaster and used as working capital to meet pre-existing financial obligations that the business could have meet before the disaster.

Economic Opportunity Loans

A Small Business Administration loan program available to small business concerns owned by, or to be established by, individuals having low incomes. The program also offers management assistance to borrowers.

Equity

The net worth of your firm, equal to the firm's monetary value minus claims against it.

Export Working Capital Program

A Small Business Administration program formed to address the export financing needs of small businesses. The program, operating in conjunction with the Export-Import Bank of the United States, handles loans under $833,333 and can guarantee pre- and post-shipment capital.

Farmers Home Administration (FmHA) Loans of the U.S. Department of Agriculture

Guaranteed long-term loans backed 90 percent by the FmHA and used as a source of start-up or working capital for residents of cities or areas located outside of major metropolitan areas having a population of 50,000 or less.

Fa-J

Fastrak Loan Program

A Small Business Administration program established to expedite the applications of small business owners applying for loans under $100,000.

Financial Ratios

Ratios measuring a company's liquidity, profitability, or performance. These ratios are often used to compare businesses in the same fields.

Fiscal Year

An accounting period of 12 consecutive months chosen by a business.

Fixed Cost

Incurred costs that are independent of sales, production, or activity levels, and that don't vary in the short-term.

FHandicapped Assistance Loan (HAL)-1

Small Business Administration handicapped assistance loans available to non-profit organizations.

Handicapped Assistance Loan (HAL)-2

Small Business Administration handicapped assistance loans available to prospective small businesses owned by a handicapped person.

Income Statement

Your statement, consisting of expenses, gains, losses, revenues and taxes, used to calculate your net income for a period.

Inventory Financing

A loan based on your unsold inventory and repaid when the inventory is sold.

Investment Tax Credit

A means of reducing federal tax liability when you purchase new equipment.

Joint Venture

An investment with another firm in a project or facility.

Journal

Your book or record of original entries of financial transactions.

L-Ma

Ledger

Your book or record of final entries containing every financial statement account.

Liability

A present obligation, resulting from past transactions or events, to transfer assets or provide services in the future.

Line of Credit

An agreement with your bank that allows your company to borrow up to a pre-determined amount at any time.

Liquid Assets

Those assets which are most easily converted to cash.

Local Development Company (502) Loans

A special Small Business Administration loan program designed for local citizen groups for the purpose of improving the economy in their area. The development company uses the loan to assist specific small businesses in either starting new businesses or purchasing or expanding existing businesses.

Location Analysis

A study of the business environment used to choose an optimal business location.

Lock-box System

A three-phase system for receiving payments: (1) the customers send payments to a post office box; (2) a local bank collects and processes the payments; and (3) the surplus funds are transferred to your firm's bank account.

Low Documentation Loan Program (LowDoc)

A Small Business Administration low documentation loan program for small businesses that guarantees a 72-hour turnaround for businesses with fewer than 100 employees and less than $5 million in gross revenues. Loan amounts are limited to $100,000.

Market Position

The position of your business or product in the marketplace as either a leader, challenger, follower, or niche.

Market Strategy

Your approach to, and policies for, successfully managing your business with respect to distribution, price, product, and promotion.

Ma-Ph

Marketable Securities

Those stocks and bonds of other companies held by your firm that you can sell for cash if needed.

Microloan Program

A Small Business Administration loan program designed to assist small businesses run by women, minorities, and low-income entrepreneurs. Microloans range from less than $100 to $25,000, and average $10,000.

Microloan Program

This program works through intermediaries to provide small loans from as little as $100 up to $25,000.

Minority Business Development Agency (MBDA)

A U.S. Department of Commerce agency that focuses on aiding minority-owned businesses.

Minority Enterprise Small Business Investment Companies (MESBIC)

Small Business Investment Companies, established under Section 301(d), designed to help small business owners and managers who are socially or economically disadvantaged (see Small Business Investment Company).

Net Income

Your revenues, minus the cost of goods sold, expenses and taxes, for a specified period.

Net Sales

Your total sales, minus returns and refunds.

Net Worth

The amount by which the assets exceed the liabilities.

Office of Advocacy

A Small Business Administration agency representing the interests of small businesses before federal agencies and consisting of four branches: Interagency Affairs, Economic Research, Information, and State and Local Affairs. The agency conducts general and specific research and is responsible for preparation of the annual report, "The President's Report on the State of Small Business."

Physical Disaster Loan

Loans to homeowners, renters, large and small business, and non-profit organizations located within disaster areas and used to repair or replace damaged or destroyed property.

Po-SBA

Pollution Control Financing

Loans to small businesses requiring long-term, fixed-rate financing to plan, design, and install pollution control facilities or equipment.

Preferred Lenders Program

A nation-wide Small Business Administration program where selected lenders manage loan paperwork and processing and service the loans, thereby trimming the paperwork and reducing the processing time.

Procurement Assistance Programs

Small Business Administration programs that help small businesses obtain a share of federal government contracts through programs such as Procurement Automated Source Systems, Prime Contracts, Subcontracts, Certificates of Competency, and Natural Resources Sales Assistance.

Procurement Automated Source System (PASS)

A Small Business Administration computerized resource base, listing small businesses, that's used by federal procurement centers and prime contractors.

Projected Cash Flow

Anticipated cash account for a given period, estimated based on the history of the business' cash flow.

Requests for Proposals (RFP)

Announcements of contracts that are open for proposals to be submitted by firms interested in bidding on the contracts.

Retained Earnings

Those earnings that aren't paid as dividends to shareholders.

Revenues

Total sales, including both "cash" and "on-account" sales.

SBA Direct Loans

Direct loans made by the Small Business Administration to applicants unable to secure an Small Business Administration guaranteed loans (no longer available).

SBA Guaranteed Loan

Loans made by private lenders that are guaranteed up to 90 percent by the Small Business Administration.

Se-Sp

Seasonal Line of Credit Loan

Loans providing short-term financing for small businesses that are active seasonally.

Seed Financing

The initial funds used to establish and operate a new business.

Service Corps of Retired Executives (SCORE)

A Small Business Administration program staffed by retired executives who volunteer their time and expertise to assist small businesses.

Small Business Answer Desk

Established in 1982 by the Office of Advocacy, the answer desk helps callers resolve questions regarding starting and managing a business, financing, and other information relevant to operating and expanding a small business. The telephone number is 1-800-368-5855.

Small Business Development Centers (SBDC)

Small Business Administration centers providing training, counseling, research, and other specialized assistance for small businesses. More than 600 locations operate free of charge.

Small Business Innovation Research Program (SBIR)

A federal grant program for small businesses that's intended to encourage innovative activities among small firms.

Small Business Investment Company (SBIC)

Privately capitalized, profit-making corporations licensed and regulated by the Small Business Administration to provide "venture" or "risk" investments to small businesses meeting their investment criteria through equity capital, extending unsecured loans, or loans that aren't fully supported by collateral.

Small General Contractor Loans

For small construction firms with short-term financing for either residential and commercial construction projects, or rehabilitating property for sale.

Specialized 7 (a): DELTA

Defense Loan and Technical Assistance is a joint SBA and DoD effort to provide financial and technical assistance to defense-dependent small firms adversely, affected by cutbacks in defense.

Specialized 7 (a): SBALowDoc

Designed to increase the availability of funds under $150,000 and streamline/expedite the loan review process.

Sp-St

Specialized 7(a): CAPLines

An umbrella program to help small businesses meet their short-term and cyclical working-capital needs with, five separate programs.

Specialized 7(a): Disabled Assistance

The SBA has not been provided funding for direct handicapped assistance loans, but such individuals are eligible for all SBA loan guaranty programs.

Specialized 7(a): Export Working Capital

Designed to provide short-term working capital to exporters in a combined effort of the SBA and the Export-Import Bank.

Specialized 7(a): International Trade

If your business is preparing to engage in or is already engaged in international trade, or is adversely affected by competition from imports, the International Trade Loan Program is designed for you.

Specialized 7(a): Minority and Women's Prequal

A pilot program that uses intermediaries to assist prospective minority and women borrowers in developing viable loan application packages and securing loans.

Specialized 7(a): Pollution Control

Designed to provide loan guarantees to eligible small business for the financing of the planning, design, or installation of a pollution control facility.

Specialized 7(a): Qualified Employee Trusts

Designed to provide financial assistance to Employee Stock Ownership Plans.

Specialized 7(a): SBAExpress

Designed to increase the capital available to businesses seeking loans up to $150,000 but is currently offered as a pilot with a limited number of lenders.

Specialized 7(a): Veteran's Loans

The SBA has not been provided funds for direct loans to Veterans, although Veterans are eligible for special considerations under SBA's guaranty loan programs.

State Business and Industrial Development Corporations (SBIDC)

Long-term loans available through state governments for either expansion of existing small businesses or for the purchase of capital equipment.

Statement of Changes in Financial Position

A statement illustrating the sources and uses of your funds during a specific period.

Su-Y

Subchapter S Corporation

An entity recognized by the IRS as a tax designation allowing small corporations to p
out income to shareholders, who then claim the income on their personal incom
taxes. This tax designation is recognized in some states. Other states don't recogni
subchapter S corporations and tax the business as any other C corporation.

Surety Bond Guarantee

Small Business Administration guarantees to a qualified surety up to 80 percent
losses for small and emerging contractors who are unable to find bonding throu
other sources.

Target Market

The market segment that you have identified as your primary customer.

U.S. Small Business Administration (SBA)

An independent federal agency, created by Congress in 1953, to help American sm
businesses to enter into and to remain in business.

Unsecured Loan

A loan that isn't backed by security or collateral.

Variable Costs

Costs that change when either your volume of sales or level of activity changes.

Veterans Franchise Program

A program co-sponsored by the Small Business Administration and Internatio
Franchise Association to reduce the capital that veterans need to buy a franchise.

Working Capital

Your current assets, minus your current liabilities. Working capital refers to the fun
available for the day-to-day operation of your business.

Y2K Action Loan Program

A loan guaranty program to address the Year 2000 computer problems of sm
businesses.

Resources

••• SBA •••

SMALL BUSINESS ADMINISTRATION
Online and telephone numbers

Main web site:
http://www.sba.gov

Form registration:
http://www.sbaonline.SBA.gov/textonly/shareware

SBA's Service Corps Of Retired Executives (SCORE):
http://www.SBA.gov/score

SBA phone numbers:
(202) 401-9600
800-697-4636
900-463-4636
E-phone assistance: (202) 205-6400

U.S. Small Business Administration Field Offices

ALABAMA
2121 8th Avenue North
Suite 200
Birmingham, AL 35203-2398
(205) 731-1344

ALASKA
222 West 8th Avenue
Anchorage, AK 99513-7559
(907) 271-4022

ARKANSAS
2120 Riverfront Drive
Little Rock, AR 72202
(501) 324-5278

ARIZONA
2828 North Central Avenue
Phoenix, AZ 85004-1025
(602) 640-2316

CALIFORNIA
2719 North Air Fresno Drive
Suite 200
Fresno, CA 93727-1547
(559) 487-5791

330 North Brand Blvd.
Glendale, CA 91203-2304
(818) 552-3210

660 J Street
Suite 215
Sacramento, CA 95814-2413
(916) 498-6410

550 West "C" Street
Suite 550
San Diego, CA 92101-3500
(619) 557-7250

455 Market Street
Suite 2200
San Francisco, CA 94105
(415) 744-2118

455 Market Street
6th Floor
San Francisco, CA 94105-2445
(415) 744-6820

200 West Santa Ana Blvd
Suite 700
Santa Ana, CA 92701
(714) 550-7420

COLORADO
721 19th Street
Suite 400
Denver, CO 80201
(303) 844-3984

721 19th Street
Suite 500
Denver, CO 80202
(303) 844-0500

CONNECTICUT
330 Main Street
Hartford CT 06106
(860) 240-4700

DELAWARE

824 North Market Street
Wilmington, DE 19801-3011
(302) 573-6294

DISTRICT OF COLUMBIA

1110 Vermont Avenue NW
Washington, DC 20005
(202) 606-4000

FLORIDA

7825 Baymeadows Way
Suite 100-B
Jacksonville, FL 32256-7504
(904) 443-1900

100 S Biscayne Blvd.
7th Floor
Miami, FL 33131
(305) 536-5521

GEORGIA

1720 Peachtree Road NW
South Tower, Suite 496
Atlanta, GA 30309-2482
(404) 347-4999

1720 Peachtree Road NW
6 th Floor
Atlanta, GA 30309-2482
(404) 347-4147

GUAM

400 Route 8
Suite 302
Mongmong, GU 96927
(671) 472-7277

HAWAII

300 Ala Moana Blvd.
Honolulu, HI 96850-4981
(808) 541-2990

IOWA

215 4th Avenue SE
Cedar Rapids, IA 52401-1806
(319) 362-6405
210 Walnut Street
Des Moines, IA 50309
(515) 284-4422

IDAHO

1020 Main Street
Boise, ID 83702
(208) 334-1696

ILLINOIS

500 West Madison Street
Chicago, IL 60661-2511
(312) 353-4528

500 West Madison Street
Chicago, IL 60661-2511
(312) 353-5000

511 West Capitol Avenue
Springfield, IL 62704
(217) 492-4416

INDIANA

429 North Pennsylvania Street
Indianapolis, IN 46204-1873
(317) 269-7272

KANSAS

100 East English Street
Wichita, KS 67202
(316) 269-6616

KENTUCKY

600 Dr. M. L. King Jr. Place
Room 188
Louisvillek, KY 40202
(502) 582-5971

LOUISIANA

365 Canal Street
New Orleans, LA 70130
(504) 589-6685

MASSACHUSETTS

10 Causeway Street
Boston, MA 02222-1093
(617) 565-8415

10 Causeway Street
Boston, MA 02222-1093
(617) 565-5590

1441 Main Street
Suite 410
Springfield, MA 01103
(413) 785-0268

MARYLAND

10 South Howard Street
Baltimore, MD 21201-2525
(410) 962-4392

MAINE

40 Western Avenue Federal Building
Room 512
Augusta, ME 04330
(207) 622-8378

MICHIGAN

McNamara Building
477 Michigan Avenue, Room 515
Detroit, MI 48226
(313) 226-6075

501 South Front Street
Marquette, MI 49855
(906) 225-1108

MINNESOTA

100 North 6 th Street
Minneapolis, MN 55403-1563
(612) 370-2324

MISSOURI

323 West 8th Street
Suite 307
Kansas City, MO 64105-1500
(816) 374-6380

323 West 8th Street
Suite 501
Kansas City, MO 64105-1500
(816) 374-6708

620 South Glenstone Street
Springfield, MO 65802-3200
(417) 864-7670

815 Olive Street
St. Louis, MO 63101
(314) 539-6600

MISSISSIPPI

2909 13th Street
Suite 203
Gulfport, MS 39501-1949
(228) 863-4449

101 W Capitol Street
Suite 400
Jackson, MS 39201
(601) 965-4378

MONTANA

301 South Park Avenue
Helena, MT 59626
(406) 441-1081

NORTH CAROLINA

200 N College Street
Suite A2015
Charlotte, NC 28202-2137
(704) 344-6563

NORTH DAKOTA

657 Second Avenue, North
Fargo, ND 58108
(701) 239-5131

NEBRASKA

11145 Mill Valley Road
Omaha, NE 68154
(402) 221-4691

NEW HAMPSHIRE

143 North Main Street
Concord, NH 03301
(603) 225-1400

NEW JERSEY

Two Gateway Center
15th Floor
Newark, NJ 07102
(973) 645-2434

NEW MEXICO

626 Silver Avenue
Albuquerque, NM 87102
(505) 346-7909

NEVADA

300 Las Vegas Blvd
Suite 1100
Las Vegas, NV 89101
(702) 388-6611

NEW YORK

111 West Huron Street
Buffalo, NY 14202
(716) 551-4301

333 East Water Street
Elmira, NY 14901
(607) 734-8130

35 Pinelawn Road
Suite 207W
Melville, NY 11747
(516) 454-0750

26 Federal Plaza
Suite 3100
New York, NY 10278
(212) 264-2454

26 Federal Plaza
Suite 3108
New York, NY 10278
(212) 264-1450

100 State Street
Rochester, NY 14614
(716) 263-6700

401 South Salina Street
5th Floor
Syracuse, NY 13202
(315) 471-9393

OHIO

525 Vine Street
Cincinnati, OH 45202
(513) 684-2814

1111 Superior Avenue
Cleveland, OH 44114-2507
(216) 522-4180

2 Nationwide Plaza
Columbus, OH 43215-2592
(614) 469-6860

OKLAHOMA

210 Park Avenue
Suite 1300
Oklahoma City, OK 73102
(405) 231-5521

OREGON

1515 SW Fifth Avenue
Portland, OR 97201-5494
(503) 326-2682

PENNSYLVANIA

100 Chestnut Street
Harrisburg, PA 17101
(717) 782-3840

900 Market Street
5th Floor
Philadelphia, PA 19107
(215) 580-2722

1000 Liberty Avenue
Federal Bldg., Room 1128
Pittsburgh, PA 15222-4004
(412) 395-6560

20 North Pennsylvania Avenue
Wilkes-Barre, PA 18791-3589
(717) 826-6497

PUERTO RICO

252 Ponce de Leon Avenue
Hato Rey, PR 00918
(809) 766-5572

RHODE ISLAND
380 Westminster Mall
Providence, RI 02903
(401) 528-4562

SOUTH CAROLINA
1835 Assembly Street
Room 358
Columbia, SC 29201
(803) 765-5377

SOUTH DAKOTA
110 South Phillips Avenue
Sioux Falls, SD 57102
(605) 330-4231

TENNESSEE
50 Vantage Way
Suite 201
Nashville, TN 37288-1500
(615) 736-5881

TEXAS
606North Carancahua
Corpus Christi, TX 78476
(512) 888-3331

4300 Amon Carter Blvd.
Dallas/Ft. Worth, TX 76155
(817) 885-6581

4300 Amon Carter Blvd.
Dallas/Ft. Worth, TX 76155
(817) 885-6500

10737 Gateway West
El Paso, TX 79935
(915) 633-7001

222 East Van Buren Street
Suite 500
Harlingen, TX 78550
(956) 427-8625

9301 Southwest Freeway
Houston, TX 77074-1591
(713) 773-6500
1205 Texas Avenue
Suite 408
Lubbock, TX 79401-2693
(806) 472-7462

727 East Durango Street
San Antonio, TX 78206
(210) 472-5900

UTAH
125 South State Street
Salt Lake City, UT 84138
(801) 524-5800

VIRGINIA
400 North 8 th Street
Suite 1150
P.O. Box 10126
Richmond, VA 23240-0126
(804) 771-2400

VIRGIN ISLANDS
3013 Golden Rock
St. Croix, VI 00820
(809) 778-5380

3800 Crown Bay
St. Thomas, VI 00801
(809) 774-8530

VERMONT

87 State Street
Montpelier, VT 05602
(802) 828-4422

WASHINGTON

1200 6th Avenue
Suite 1700
Seattle, WA 98101-1128
(206) 553-7310

1200 6th Avenue
Suite 1805
Seattle, WA 98101-1128
(206) 553-5676

801 West Riverside Avenue
Suite 200
Spokane, WA 99201-0901
(509) 353-2800

WISCONSIN

212 East Washington Avenue
Room 213
Madison, WI 53703
(608) 264-5261

Henry S. Reuss Federal Plaza
310 West Wisconsin Avenue
Suite 400
Milwaukee, WI 53203
(414) 297-3941

WEST VIRGINIA

405 Capitol Street
Suite 412
Charleston, WV 25301
(304) 347-5220

Federal Center
Suite 330
320 West Pike Street
Clarksburg, WV 26301
(304) 623-5631

WYOMING

100 East B Street
Federal Building, Room 4001
P. O. Box 2839
Casper, WY 82602
(307) 261-6500

••• Organizations •••

American Accounting Association
5717 Bessie Drive
Sarasota, FL, 34233
(813) 921-7747

American Advertising Federation
1101 Vermont Avenue, Suite 500
Washington, D.C., 20008
(202) 898-0090

American Association for Public
Opinion Research
19 Chamber Street, P.O. Box 17
Princeton, NJ, 08542
(609) 924-8670

American Association in Insurance
Services
1035 South York Road
Bensenville, IL, 60106
(708) 595-3225

American Association of Inventors
2309 State
Saginaw, MI, 48602
(517) 799-8208

American Automotive Leasing
Association
1001 Connecticut Avenue, NW
Suite 1201,
Washington, D.C., 20036
(202) 223-2600

American Bankers Association
1120 Connecticut Avenue NW
Washington, D.C., 20036
(202) 663-5000

American Bar Association
750 North Lake Shore Drive
Chicago, IL 60611
(312) 988-5000

American Institute of Certified Public
Accountants
1211 Avenue of the Americas
New York, NY, 10036
(212) 596-6200

American Insurance Association
1130 Connecticut Avenue NW
Suite 1000
Washington, D.C., 20036,
(202) 828-7100

American League of Financial
Institutions
900 19th Street NW
Washington, D.C., 20006
(202) 628-5624

American Management Association
135 West 50th Street
New York, NY, 40020
(212) 586-8100

American Marketing Association
250 South Wacker Drive, Suite200
Chicago, IL, 60606
(312) 648-0536

American Production and Inventory
Control Society
500 West Annandale Road
Falls Church, VA, 22046-4274
(703) 237-8344

American Society of Inventors
1 Meridan Plaza, Suite 900
Philadelphia, PA, 19102
(215) 546-6601

American Telemarketing Association
444 North Larchmont Boulevard
Suite 200
Los Angeles, CA, 90004
(213) 463-2330

Association of National Advertisers
155 East 44th Street
New York, NY, 10017
(212) 697-5950

Association of Sales Administration
Managers
P.O. Box 735
Harrson, NJ, 07029
(201) 481-4800

Association of Small Business
Development Centers
1050 17th Street NW, Suite 810
Washington, DC, 10036
(202) 887-2299

Association of Tax Consultants
1313 12th Avenue SE, Suite 100
Portland, OR, 97214
(505) 238-0834

Cable TV. Advertising Bureau
757 Third Avenue, 5th Floor
New York, NY, 10017
(212) 751-7770

Center for Entrepreneurial
Management, Inc.
180 Varick Street
New York, NY, 10014
(212) 633-0060

CPA Associates
230 Park Avenue, Suite 1545,
New York, NY, 10169
(212) 818-9700

CWI: Credit Professionals
50 Crestwood Executive Center
Suite 204
Street Louis, MO, 63126
(314) 842-6280

Dunn & Bradstreet Corp Credit
Services
1 Diamond Hill Road
Murray Hill, NJ, 17974-0000
(908) 665-5000

Equipment Leasing Association of
America
1300 North 17th Street, Suite 1010
Arlington, VA, 22209
(703) 527-8655

Financial Executives Institute
10 Madison Avenue, P.O. Box 1938
Morristown, NJ, 07962-1938
(201) 898-4649

Financial Management Association
University of South Florida
School of Business
Tampa, FL, 33620
(813) 974-3318

Franchise Consultants International
Association
5147 South Angela Road
Memphis, TN, 38117
(901) 761-3085

Independent Accountants
International
9200 S. Dateland Boulevard, Suite 510
Miami, FL, 33156
(305) 670-0580

Independent Bankers Association of
America
One Thomas Circle NW, Suite 950
Washington, D.C., 20005
(202) 659-8111

Industrial Development Research
Council
40 Technology Park/Atlanta, Suite 200
Norcross, GA, 30092
(404) 446-6996

Institute of Chartered Financial
Analysts
P.O. Box 3668
Charlottesville, VA, 22908
(804) 977-6600

Institute of Tax Consultants
7500 212th Street SW, Suite 205
Edmonds, WA, 98026
(206) 774-3521

Insurance Information Institute
110 William Street
New York, NY, 10038
(212) 669-9200

International Credit Association
243 North Lindbergh Boulevard
St. Louis, MO, 63141
(314) 991-3030

International Franchise Association
1350 New York Avenue NW, Suite 900
Washington, D.C., 20005
(202) 628-8000

International Institute of Site Planning
715 G Street SE
Washington, D.C., 20003
(202) 546-2322

International Internet Association(IIA)
2020 Pennsylvania Avenue NW
Suite 852
Washington, D.C., 20006
(202) 387-5445

International Licensing Industry
Merchandiser's Association
350 Fifth Avenue, Suite 6210
New York, NY, 10118
(212) 244-1944

Invention Marketing Institute
345 West Cypress Street
Glendale, CA, 91204
(818) 246-6540

Inventor's Awareness Group
171 Interstate Drive, Suite 6
West Springfield, MA, 01089-4533
(413) 739-3938

Marketing Research Association
2189 Salas Deane Highway
Rocky Hill, CT, 06067
(203) 257-4008

Marketing Science Institute
1000 Massachusetts Avenue
Cambridge, MA, 02138
(617) 491-2060

MoneySoft, Inc.
One E. Camelback Road, Suite 550
Phoenix, AZ, 85012
(602) 226-7719

National Association for the Self-
Employed
9151 Precinct Line Road
Hurst, TX, 76054
(817) 656-6313

National Association of Development
Companies
444 North Capital Street NW
Suite 630
Washington, D.C., 20001
(202) 624-7806

National Association of Investment
Companies
1111 14th Street NW, Suite 700
Washington, D.C., 20005
(202) 289-4336

National Association of Small Business
Investment Companies
1199 North Fairfax Street, Suite 200
Alexandria, VA, 22314
(703) 683-1601

National Association of Tax
Consultants
454 North 13th Street
San Jose, CA, 95112
(408) 298-1458

National Business Incubation
Association
One President Street
Athens, OH, 45701
(614) 593-4331

National Commercial Finance
Association
25 West 34th Street, Suite 1815
New York, NY, 10122
(212) 594-3490

National Congress of Inventor
Organizations
727 North 600 West
Logan, UT, 84321
(801) 753-0888

National Corporate Cash Management
Association
7315 Wisconsin Avenue
Suite 1250 West
Bethesda, MD, 20814
(301) 907-2862

National Council of Savings
Institutions
900 19th Street NW
Washington, D.C., 20006
(202) 857-3100

National Insurance Association
P.O. Box 158544
Chicago, IL, 60615
(313) 924-3308

National Inventors Foundation
345 West Cypress Street
Glendale, CA, 91204
(818) 246-6540

National Management Association
2210 Arbor Boulevard
Dayton, OH, 45439
(513) 294-0421

National Office Systems Association
P.O. Box 8187
Silver Spring, MD, 21917
(301) 589-8125

National Register Publishing
121 Chanlon Road
New Providence, NJ, 07974
(800) 323-3288

National Small Business United
1155 15th Street NW, Suite 710
Washington, D.C., 20005
(202) 593-8830

National Vehicle Leasing Association
P.O. Box 281230
San Francisco, CA, 94128
(415) 548-9135

National Venture Capital Association
1655 North Fort Myer Drive, Suite 700
Arlington, VA, 22209
(703) 351-5269

Newspaper Association of America
711 Third Avenue
New York, NY, 10017
(212) 856-6300

Outdoor Advertising Association of
America
12 East 49th Street, 22nd Floor
New York, NY, 10017
(212) 688-3667

Point-of-Purchase Advertising Institute
66 North Van Brunt Street
Englewood, NJ, 07631
(201) 894-8899

Radio Advertising Bureau
304 Park Avenue South
New York, NY, 10010
(212) 254-4800

Risk and Insurance Management
Society
205 East 42nd Street
New York, NY, 10017
(212) 286-9292

Sales and Marketing Executives
International
Statler Office Tower, Suite 458
Cleveland, OH, 44115
(216) 771-6650

Self-Insurance Institute of America
P.O. Box 157466
Santa Ana, CA, 92705
(714) 261-2553

Small Business Network
10451 Millrun Circle, Suite 400
Owensville, MD, 21117
(410) 581-1373

Small Business Service Bureau
554 Main Street
Worchester, MA, 01601
(508) 756-3513

Small Business Support Center
Association
8600 Bissonnet, Suite 570
Houston, TX, 77074
(713) 271-4232

Society of Risk Management
Consultants
300 Park Avenue
New York, NY, 10022
(800) 765-SRMC

Thomas Publishing Company
Five Penn Plaza
New York, NY, 10001
(212) 695-0500

Vankirk Business Information
2800 Shirlington Road, Suite 904
Arlington, VA, 22206
(703) 379-9200

••• Online Resources •••

◆ About.com
   http://www.sbinformation.about.com

◆ AltaVista Small Business
   http://altavista.looksmart.com/eus1/eus65300/eus65319/r?l&izf&

◆ America's Business Funding Directory
   http://www.business finance.com/search.asp

◆ AOL.COM Business & Careers
   http://www.aol.com/webcenters/workplace/home.adp

◆ BizMove.com
   http://www.bizmove.com

◆ Biztalk.com Small Business Community
   http://www.biztalk.com

◆ Bplans.com!
   http://www.bplans.com

◆ BusinessTown.Com
   http://www.businesstown.com

◆ Council of Better Business Bureaus, Inc.
   http://www.bbb.org

◆ Education Index, Business Resources
   http://www.educationindex.com/bus

◆ Electric Library Business Edition
   http://www.business.elibrary.com

◆ EntrepreneurMag.com
   http://www.entrepreneurmag.com

◆ **Federal Trade Commission-Franchise and Business Opportunities**
http://www.ftc.gov/bcp/menu-fran.htm

◆ **HotBot Directory/Small Business**
http://directory.hotbot.com/Business/Small_Business

◆ **Inc. Online**
http://www.inc.com

◆ **Infoseek: Small Business**
http://infoseek.go.com/Center/Business/Small_business

◆ **Internal Revenue Service**
http://www.irs.ustreas.gov/prod/cover.html

◆ **International Finance & Commodities Institute**
http://finance.wat.ch/IFCI

◆ **LNET-LLC-The Limited Liability Companies and Partnerships Conference**
http://www.stcl.edu/lnet-llc/lnet-llc.html

◆ **Limited Liability Company Website**
http://www.llcweb.com

◆ **Lycos Directory: Small Business**
http://dir.lycos.com/Business/Small_Business

◆ **Netscape Women in Business**
http://women.netscape.com/smallbusiness

◆ **National Association of Small Business Investment Companies**
http://www.nasbic.org

◆ **National Foundation for Women Business Owners (NFWBO)**
http://www.nfwbo.org

◆ **National Small Business Development Center (SBDC) Research
Network**
http://www.smallbiz.suny.edu

◆ **National Small Business Network Resource Directory**
http://businessknowhow.net/Directory/bkhDindex.asp

◆ **National Small Business United**
http://www.nsbu.org

◆ **North American Securities Administrators Association (NASAA)**
http://www.nasaa.org

◆ **Occupational Safety and Health Administration (OSHA)**
http://www.osha.gov

◆ **Service Core of Retired Executives**
http://www.score.org

◆ **Small Business Advisor**
http://www.isquare.com

◆ **Small Business Assistance, Environmental Protection Agency**
http://es.epa.gov/new/business/business.html

◆ **Small Business Innovation Research (SBIR) Program**
http://es.epa.gov/business/index.html

◆ **Small Business Primer**
http://www.ces.ncsu.edu/depts/fcs/business/welcome.html

◆ **Small Business Resource**
http://www.irl.co.uk/sbr

◆ **Small Business Taxes & Management**
http://www.smbiz.com

◆ **Smalloffice.com**
http://www.smalloffice.com

◆ **Tax and Accounting Sites Directory**
http://www.taxsites.com

◆ **U.S. Business Advisor**
http://www.business.gov

◆ **U.S. Chamber of Commerce**
http://www.uschamber.org/smallbiz/index.html

◆ **U.S. Equal Employment Opportunity Commission's (EEOC)**
http://www.eeoc.gov

◆ **U.S. Government Printing Office-Small Business**
http://www.access.gpo.gov/su_docs/sale/sb-307.html

◆ **U.S. Small Business Administration**
http://www.sbaonline.sba.gov

◆ **U.S. Treasury Department-Business Services**
http://www.ustreas.gov/busserv.html

◆ **Webcrawler: Small Business**
http://quicken.webcrawler.com/small_business

◆ **Yahoo! Business and Economy: Marketing**
http://dir.yahoo.com/Business_and_Economy/Marketing

◆ **Yahoo! Small Business**
http://smallbusiness.yahoo.com

••• Legal Search Engines •••

- **All Law**
  http://www.alllaw.com

- **American Law Sources On Line**
  http://www.lawsource.com/also/searchfm.htm

- **Catalaw**
  http://www.catalaw.com

- **FindLaw**
  http://www.findlaw.com

- **InternetOracle**
  http://www.internetoracle.com/legal.htm

- **LawAid**
  http://www.lawaid.com/search.html

- **LawCrawler**
  http://www.lawcrawler.com

- **LawEngine, The**
  http://www.fastsearch.com/law

- **LawRunner**
  http://www.lawrunner.com

- **'Lectric Law Library™**
  http://www.lectlaw.com

◆ **Legal Search Engines**
   http://www.dreamscape.com/frankvad/search.legal.html

◆ **LEXIS/NEXIS Communications Center**
   http://www.lexis-nexis.com/lncc/general/search.html

◆ **Meta-Index for U.S. Legal Research**
   http://gsulaw.gsu.edu/metaindex

◆ **Seamless Website, The**
   http://seamless.com

◆ **USALaw**
   http://www.usalaw.com/linksrch.cfm

◆ **WestLaw**
   http://westdoc.com (Registered users only. Fee paid service.)

••• State Bar Associations •••

ALABAMA

Alabama State Bar
415 Dexter Avenue
Montgomery, AL 36104
mailing address:
PO Box 671
Montgomery, AL 36101
(334) 269-1515
http://www.alabar.org

ALASKA

Alaska Bar Association
510 L Street No. 602
Anchorage, AK 99501
mailing address:
PO Box 100279
Anchorage, AK 99510
http://www.alaskabar.org

ARIZONA

State Bar of Arizona
111 West Monroe
Phoenix, AZ 85003-1742
(602) 252-4804
http://www.azbar.org

ARKANSAS

Arkansas Bar Association
400 West Markham
Little Rock, AR 72201
(501) 375-4605
http://www.arkbar.org

CALIFORNIA

State Bar of California
555 Franklin Street
San Francisco, CA 94102
(415) 561-8200
http://www.calbar.org

Alameda County Bar
Association
http://www.acbanet.org

COLORADO

Colorado Bar Association
No. 950, 1900 Grant Street
Denver, CO 80203
(303) 860-1115
http://www.cobar.org

CONNECTICUT

Connecticut Bar Association
101 Corporate Place
Rocky Hill, CT 06067-1894
(203) 721-0025
http://www.ctbar.org

DELAWARE

Delaware State Bar Association
1225 King Street, 10th floor
Wilmington, DE 19801
(302) 658-5279
(302) 658-5278 (lawyer referral
service)
http://www.dsba.org

DISTRICT OF COLUMBIA

District of Columbia Bar
1250 H Street, NW, 6th Floor
Washington, DC 20005
(202) 737-4700

Bar Association of the District
of Columbia
1819 H Street, NW, 12th floor
Washington, DC 20006-3690
(202) 223-6600
http://www.badc.org

FLORIDA

The Florida Bar
The Florida Bar Center
650 Apalachee Parkway
Tallahassee, FL 32399-2300
(850) 561-5600
http://www.flabar.org

GEORGIA

State Bar of Georgia
800 The Hurt Building
50 Hurt Plaza
Atlanta, GA 30303
(404) 527-8700
http://www.gabar.org

HAWAII

Hawaii State Bar Association
1136 Union Mall
Penthouse 1
Honolulu, HI 96813
(808) 537-1868
http://www.hsba.org

IDAHO

Idaho State Bar
PO Box 895
Boise, ID 83701
(208) 334-4500
http://www2.state.id.us/isb

ILLINOIS

Illinois State Bar Association
424 South Second Street
Springfield, IL 62701
(217) 525-1760
http://www.illinoisbar.org

INDIANA

Indiana State Bar Association
230 East Ohio Street
Indianapolis, IN 46204
(317) 639-5465
http://www.ai.org/isba

IOWA

Iowa State Bar Association
521 East Locust
Des Moines, IA 50309
(515) 243-3179
http://www.iowabar.org

KANSAS

Kansas Bar Association
1200 Harrison Street
Topeka, KS 66612-1806
(785) 234-5696
http://www.ksbar.org

KENTUCKY

Kentucky Bar Association
514 West Main Street
Frankfort, KY 40601-1883
(502) 564-3795
http://www.kybar.org

LOUISIANA

Louisiana State Bar Association
601 St. Charles Avenue
New Orleans, LA 70130
(504) 566-1600
http://www.lsba.org

MAINE

Maine State Bar Association
124 State Street
PO Box 788
Augusta, ME 04330
(207) 622-7523
http://www.mainebar.org

MARYLAND

Maryland State Bar Association
520 West Fayette Street
Baltimore, MD 21201
(301) 685-7878
http://www.msba.org/msba

MASSACHUSETTS

Massachusetts Bar Association
20 West Street
Boston, MA 02111
(617) 542-3602
(617) 542-9103 (lawyer referral service)
http://www.massbar.org

MICHIGAN

State Bar of Michigan
306 Townsend Street
Lansing, MI 48933-2083
(517) 372-9030
http://www.michbar.org

MINNESOTA

Minnesota State Bar Association
514 Nicollet Mall
Minneapolis, MN 55402
(612) 333-1183
http://www.mnbar.org

MISSISSIPPI

The Mississippi Bar
643 No. State Street
Jackson, Mississippi 39202
(601) 948-4471
http://www.msbar.org

MISSOURI

The Missouri Bar
P.O. Box 119, 326 Monroe
Jefferson City, Missouri 65102
(314) 635-4128
http://www.mobar.org

MONTANA

State Bar of Montana
46 North Main
PO Box 577
Helena, MT 59624
(406) 442-7660
http://www.montanabar.org

NEBRASKA

Nebraska State Bar Association
635 South 14th Street, 2nd floor
Lincoln, NE 68508
(402) 475-7091
http://www.nebar.com

NEVADA

State Bar of Nevada
201 Las Vegas Blvd.
Las Vegas, NV 89101
(702) 382-2200
http://www.nvbar.org

NEW HAMPSHIRE
New Hampshire Bar
Association
112 Pleasant Street
Concord, NH 03301
(603) 224-6942
http://www.nhbar.org

NEW JERSEY
New Jersey State Bar
Association
One Constitution Square
New Brunswick, NJ 08901-1500
(908) 249-5000

NEW MEXICO
State Bar of New Mexico
5121 Masthead N.E.
Albuquerque, NM 87125
mailing address:
PO Box 25883
Albuquerque, NM 87125
(505) 843-6132
http://www.nmbar.org

NEW YORK
New York State Bar Association
One Elk Street
Albany, NY 12207
(518) 463-3200
http://www.nysba.org

NORTH CAROLINA
North Carolina State Bar
208 Fayetteville Street Mall
Raleigh, NC 27601
mailing address:
PO Box 25908
Raleigh, NC 27611
(919) 828-4620

North Carolina Bar Association
1312 Annapolis Drive
Raleigh, NC 27608
mailing address:
PO Box 3688
Cary, NC 27519-3688
(919) 677-0561
http://www.ncbar.org

NORTH DAKOTA
State Bar Association of North
Dakota
515 1/2 East Broadway, suite 101
Bismarck, ND 58501
mailing address:
PO Box 2136
Bismarck, ND 58502
(701) 255-1404

OHIO
Ohio State Bar Association
1700 Lake Shore Drive
Columbus, OH 43204
mailing address:
PO Box 16562
Columbus, OH 43216-6562
(614) 487-2050
http://www.ohiobar.org

OKLAHOMA
Oklahoma Bar Association
1901 North Lincoln
Oklahoma City, OK 73105
(405) 524-2365
http://www.okbar.org

OREGON

Oregon State Bar
5200 S.W. Meadows Road
PO Box 1689
Lake Oswego, OR 97035-0889
(503) 620-0222
http://www.osbar.org

PENNSYLVANIA

Pennsylvania Bar Association
100 South Street
PO Box 186
Harrisburg, PA 17108
(717) 238-6715
http://www.pabar.org

Pennsylvania Bar Institute
http://www.pbi.org

PUERTO RICO

Puerto Rico Bar Association
PO Box 1900
San Juan, Puerto Rico 00903
(787) 721-3358

RHODE ISLAND

Rhode Island Bar Association
115 Cedar Street
Providence, RI 02903
(401) 421-5740
http://www.ribar.org

SOUTH CAROLINA

South Carolina Bar
950 Taylor Street
PO Box 608
Columbia, SC 29202
(803) 799-6653
http://www.scbar.org

SOUTH DAKOTA

State Bar of South Dakota
222 East Capitol
Pierre, SD 57501
(605) 224-7554
http://www.sdbar.org

TENNESSEE

Tennessee Bar Assn
3622 West End Avenue
Nashville, TN 37205
(615) 383-7421
http://www.tba.org

TEXAS

State Bar of Texas
1414 Colorado
PO Box 12487
Austin, TX 78711
(512) 463-1463
http://www.texasbar.com/start.htm

UTAH

Utah State Bar
645 South 200 East, Suite 310
Salt Lake City, UT 84111
(801) 531-9077
http://www.utahbar.org

VERMONT

Vermont Bar Association
PO Box 100
Montpelier, VT 05601
(802) 223-2020
http://www.vtbar.org

VIRGINIA

Virginia State Bar
707 East Main Street, suite 1500
Richmond, VA 23219-0501
(804) 775-0500

Virginia Bar Association
701 East Franklin St., Suite 1120
Richmond, VA 23219
(804) 644-0041
http://www.vbar.org

VIRGIN ISLANDS

Virgin Islands Bar Association
P.O. Box 4108
Christiansted, Virgin Islands
00822
(340) 778-7497

WASHINGTON

Washington State Bar
Association
500 Westin Street
2001 Sixth Avenue
Seattle, WA 98121-2599
(206) 727-8200
http://www.wsba.org

WEST VIRGINIA

West Virginia State Bar
2006 Kanawha Blvd. East
Charleston, WV 25311
(304) 558-2456
http://www.wvbar.org

West Virginia Bar Association
904 Security Building
100 Capitol Street
Charleston, WV 25301
(304) 342-1474

WISCONSIN

State Bar of Wisconsin
402 West Wilson Street
Madison, WI 53703
(608) 257-3838
*http://www.wisbar.org/
home.htm*

WYOMING

Wyoming State Bar
500 Randall Avenue
Cheyenne, WY 82001
PO Box 109
Cheyenne, WY 82003
(307) 632-9061
http://www.wyomingbar.org

Appendices

LIST OF TABLES

Table 1.1—Small Business Administration Loan Programs.

•	7(a) Guaranteed Loan Program
•	7(a) Loan Guaranty
•	8(a) Participant Loan Program
•	Certified Development Company (504 Loan) Program
•	Economic Injury Disaster Loan
•	Economic Opportunity Loan
•	Export Working Capital Program
•	Fastrak Loan Program
•	Handicapped Assistance Loan 1 and 2
•	Local Development Company (502) Loans
•	Low Documentation Loan Program (LowDoc)
•	Microloan Program
•	Physical Disaster Loan
•	Pollution Control Financing
•	Seasonal Line of Credit Loan
•	Y2K Action Loan

Table 1.2—Specialized Small Business Administration Programs.

•	Specialized 7(a): DELTA—Defense Loan and Technical Assistance
•	Specialized 7(a): SBALowDoc
•	Specialized 7(a): CAPLines
•	Specialized 7(a): Disable Assistance
•	Specialized 7(a): Export Working Capital
•	Specialized 7(a): International Trade
•	Specialized 7(a): Minority and Women's Prequal
•	Specialized 7(a): Pollution Control
•	Specialized 7(a): Qualified Employee Trusts
•	Specialized 7(a): SBAExpress
•	Specialized 7(a): Veteran's Loans

Table 1.3—Other Government Loans Available To Small Businesses.

•	Department of Energy Loan
•	Department of Housing and Urban Development Loan
•	Department of Interior Grant
•	Economic Development Administration Loan of the U.S. Department of Commerce
•	Farmers Home Administration (FmHA) Loans of the U.S. Department of Agriculture

Table 2.1—Loan Package Elements and General Proposal Outline.

Loan Package Elements
• Company or business history (may not apply to a start-up business)
• Owner and manager profiles (including resumes and organization chart)
• Proposed business description (operations)
• Marketing
• Financial information
• Purpose of loan
• Amount of loan and use of loan proceeds
• Loan repayment
• Small business administration forms
• Other supporting information

Table 2.2—Loan Package Elements and Suggested Order of Preparation.

Groups	Elements	Chapter	Suggested Order of Preparation[(1)]
Tax, Legal, and Other Information	• Tax information • Legal information • Other supporting information	2	**First**, **gather** your information before you begin developing your loan package, including any personal records you might need.
SBA Forms	• SBA Standard Form 4 • SBA Form 912 • SBA Schedule of Collateral (Exhibit A) • SBA Form 413 • SBA Form 1624 • SBA Form 1846 • SBA Form 159 • IRS Form 4506	5	**Second**, now that you're organized, retrieve the information needed to complete the required SBA forms. By gathering this information, you'll begin to develop a feeling for your loan proposal. Using a pencil, see how much of each form you're able to complete with your existing information. This will also indicate where you have gaps in your information.
Owner and Organization Descriptions	• Company history (Personal history for start-up)	3	**Third**, begin to draft a description of your company's history, or in the case of a start-up, how you decided to enter this business venture.

162

	• Resumes • Owner and manager profiles • Organization chart	2	**Fourth**, because this discussion applies to a start-up business, there is no existing organization to reveal. In this situation, well-written owner and manager profiles (including individual resumes and an organization chart) will be essential in supporting your application.
	• Business description (operations)	3	**Fifth**, begin to develop a narrative of how the business will operate (business description).
	• Marketing	3	**Sixth**, once you have completed step 5, think about how you'll market your product or service and begin to develop a narrative of your marketing plans for the business.
Financial Matters	• Financial summary of company	4	**Seventh**, summarize, in one or two sentences, each financial presentation listed below.
	• Balance sheet • Profit and loss statement	4	**May not be relevant to a start-up business.**
	• Personal financial statement • Cash-flow projections • Purpose of loan • Amount of loan and use of proceeds • Loan repayment	4	**Eighth**, gather the information needed for the necessary financial forms and prepare them.

Note: (1) You may begin developing you loan proposal package by selecting any group of elements with which you're comfortable.

Table 2.3—Typical Legal Information.

Purchases and Leases
• Real estate purchase contracts
• Real and personal property titles
• Purchase and lease agreements on property and equipment
• Any other pertinent purchase or lease agreements
Agreements or Contracts
• Licensing agreements
• Operating agreements
• Trade purchase agreements
• Shareholder agreements
Licenses and Permits
• Business licenses, required by your state or county (e.g., sales tax, unemployment filing, withholding, or other)
• Professional licenses (e.g., certified public accountant, real estate broker, or other)
Business Documents
• Articles of incorporation, partnership agreements, or other documents identifying legal entities
• Trademarks or trade names and patents
• Any other relevant business documents

Table 2.4—Typical Supporting Information.

Items
• Commitments from prospective customers or clients and their letters of intent to do business with your proposed firm
• Purchase orders from prospective customers or clients
• Letters of reference form business contacts
• Letters of reference from personal contacts
• Letters of credit from vendors
• Map of proposed business location
• Photographs
• Area economic studies
• Environmental survey information, if purchasing possibly contaminated property
• Marketing information

Table 2.5—General Steps in Preparing or Revising a Resume.

Step No. 1—Gather Information
Gather the following relevant background information: • Work experience • Volunteer experience • Education • Licensing, certification, special skills, and training • Military experience • Memberships and activities • Awards and honors
Step No. 2—Select a Format
Chronological Format—This traditional format emphasizes work history and is organized as follows: • Personal identifying information (name, address, telephone number) • Personal objective (sentence or paragraph) • Summary of skills and/or qualifications • Professional experience • Education • Memberships, activities, honors, or other relevant information
Functional Format—This format emphasizes qualifications, experience, and accomplishments grouped according to skills and is organized as follows: • Identifying information (name, address, telephone number) • Objective • Summary of skills and/or qualifications • Skills and achievements • Education, activities, honors, or other relevant information
Step No. 3—Prepare a Rough Draft
• Emphasize the most relevant experience and qualifications (you may not use all of the information gathered in Step No. 1). • Be clear and concise—focus on the information supportive of your loan application. • Be attentive to content (rough drafts aren't perfect—perfection comes later).
Step No. 4—Design the Presentation
Check your word processing program for resume layout options or create your own easy-to-read layout.
Step No. 5—Edit and Correct the Draft
• Prepare and print a copy of your resume. • Edit your resume—if it's too long, condense it to one page (two at the most). • Double check your facts and figures for accuracy.
Step No. 6—Proofread
Make sure your resume is completely free of errors.

Table 3.1—Typical Information Presented in a Business Operations Description.

What	Example
What is the nature of the industry you propose to enter? This will differ for manufacturing, retail, and services business. (Service business).	Healthful Way, Inc., proposes to provide home health-care services for any type of illness for patients located within a 60-mile radius of the city center. The owners have chosen a unique niche in the market and have taken a leadership position in servicing long-term care for patients entering the managed health-care system.
What is the type of business proposed, e.g., manufacturing, retail, or service? (Manufacturing business).	The proposed manufacturing company will be a small family-owned and operated minority business that fabricates unique rugs for clients based upon original or existing designs.
What is the purpose of the proposed business? Be specific. (Service business)	The purpose of the proposed company is to provide specific programming, such as Level II education and therapy, relapse prevention, domestic violence, anger management, and cognitive behavioral therapy, for individuals on parole from corrective facilities.
What is the status of the proposed business? For a business start-up, the status of the business will be "new" rather than "existing." (Manufacturing business).	The proposed firm, Looking Glass Publishing, Inc., is a newly formed entity dedicated to publishing quality fiction for children.
What is the type of entity, e.g., sole proprietorship, partnership, corporation, LLC? (Any type of business).	The business will be incorporated as Jackson Enterprises, Inc., and will be jointly owned by Mr. Ammon Jackson, with 60 percent interest ownership, and Mr. Joseph Andrews, with a 40 percent interest.
What are the proposed products or services? (This example is for a service business. If you're planning a retail business, attach catalogs or itemize the products in a table format).	ACE Auto Service, Inc., will specialize in providing emissions testing for older cars. Additionally, ACE will manage a small fleet of U-Haul® rental vehicles ranging in size from mini-vans to 16-ft trucks.
What are the components ("tools") of the proposed business? This will vary depending upon the type of business. Use tables if you have a long equipment list. If you're proposing a manufacturing business, the list of components may be extensive. (Service business).	Each of the three proposed facilities, consisting of approximately 1,500-square feet of meeting and office space, has lighted parking areas to ensure client safety for evening meetings. The centers will be fully equipped with hand-held breathalyzers; urine testing supplies; computers and card reading devices; and facilities necessary to conduct group and individual sessions, employment training, and administration.

Where	Example
Where will the proposed business be located and for how long? Location is driven by the type of business and local code. Thoroughly consider your intended market prior to selecting a location. As they say in real estate, the three most import factors in determining property value are location, location, and location. This is also true for your business. (Service business).	Mr. Wan's proposed restaurant location is near the corner of 17th Avenue and Main Street. When Mr. Wan began scouting locations, he was attracted to this high-traffic area in close proximity to governmental and commercial facilities. Other establishments located in the same block include used furniture and comic book dealers, a convenience store, and a candy shop. The proposed location is available to Mr. Wan for a five-year lease with an option to renew at the end of the five-year term.

When	Example
When will the business be open? (Any type of business).	The business, staffed by two full-time employees, will be operated Monday through Friday and is open to the public from 7:30 a.m. to 4:30 p.m. After normal business hours, a staff member will be on call to manage emergency situations.
When will the business achieve proposed milestones? If tables, graphics or timelines are useful in demonstrating your schedule, use them to your advantage. (Manufacturing business).	Looking Glass Publishing's proposed timeline is shown in Table A [not shown]. Major milestones are to accept delivery of equipment after the loan is closed, and to publish the first work 60 days after the equipment is installed and operational.

Who	Example
Who is your competition? Make sure you know your competition and provide details. If you're planning to enter a highly competitive field, your homework in this area must be solid. (Service business).	Two other restaurants serving authentic Mexican food, Ranchers Inn and Tex-Mex Restaurant, are located three miles south of El Tacorito's proposed location. A Western Sizzlin' Steak House is located north of the proposed location. El Tacorito's location will be favorably situated within two blocks of four motels to receive an influx of tourists in addition to local patrons.

Why	Example
Why will the business be successful? Describe your competitive edge, unique features, and customer benefits (Retail business).	Fantastic Boxes, Ltd., offers a unique service that is duplicated no where else in the state. The business proposes to place locked job boxes stocked with fastening devices, such as those shown in the attached catalog, at client locations and periodically replenish the stock. The company also plans to respond to individual client orders for unusual fastening devices or materials that aren't initially included in the stocked job boxes.

How	Example
How many employees will you need to start the business? How many employees will you need to accommodate anticipated growth during the first year of business? (Service business).	El Tocorito, Inc.'s, proposed staff will consist of one head chef, two assistant chefs, one head waitperson, four waitpersons, one cashier, and one hostess. By the end of the first year, anticipated growth will permit the addition of one assistant chef and two waitpersons.
How will the business operate? This will vary depending upon whether the business is a manufacturing, retail, or service company. (Manufacturing business).	Once the client has selected the materials available through either Custom Rugs, Ltd., or another source and has paid a 50 percent deposit, rugs are created following these general steps: 1. Either prepare a freehand drawing of the design, select an existing design, or create a design. 2. Scan the freehand drawing into the computer. 3. Refine the drawing using specialized computer programs. Trace the drawing on the screen and redraw the picture to smooth the design. 4. Print the drawing for approval by the client. 5. Lay out the pieces for automated cutting that maximizes the use of each piece of carpet. 6. Set the program and cut the pieces. 7. Transfer the instructions to the cutting machine. 8. Assemble the pieces and seam them together on the back side of the rug using the hot-melt seam procedure. 9. Bevel the design on the front side of the rug. 10. Apply secondary backing and bind the edges. 11. Vacuum the rug and notify the client.
How will you make the business profitable? (Service business).	Mobile Lube, Inc., plans to ensure maximum profitability by efficiently scheduling appointments on evenings and weekends or at other times convenient for our clients. The company also plans bulk purchases as a more cost-effective means of acquiring materials and supplies.
How will you manage your vendors? (Retail business).	Fantastic Boxes, Ltd., has written agreements with suppliers to maintain inventory. Each vendor has agreed to extend credit during the first two months following business start-up.

	Major suppliers of pre-packaged and bulk items include:
	• ABC Warehouse, Denver, Colorado—this company is a manufacturer's representative. Fantastic Boxes, Ltd., expects to purchase fasteners three to seven times per week. Monthly purchases are expected to average $3,750 during the first year.
	• DOM Fasteners, Inc., Los Angeles, California—Fantastic Boxes, Ltd., expects to order bulk stock every three to six months for repackaging. A typical bulk order may consist of 20,000 quarter-20 hex nuts costing $60 per order. Fantastic Boxes, Ltd., will repackage the bulk items into smaller packages.

Table 3.2—Typical Information Presented in a Marketing Plan.

Who	Example
To whom are you planning on selling your products or services? Define your target audience—the buyers/customers/clients. (Service business).	Sushi, Inc., plans to attract customers who enjoy Japanese food or who are visiting from Japan. Other targeted customers drawn from the area include members of the state legislature, business people, and lawyers.
Where	**Example**
Where is your target audience located? (Describe the demographics).	Home health-care service is a growth industry fueled by the demographics of an aging population. Healthful Match, Inc., plans to serve long-term Medicare and Medicaid patients throughout the metropolitan area, filling a unique niche for this population.
How	**Example**
How much of the market share can you expect to capture during your first year of business? (Be realistic—expect a small share in a competitive market).	The overall home health-care industry in the metropolitan area is valued at $2 billion annually. The dominant agency controls 65 percent of the local market. The next largest agency controls 15 percent and another agency controls 10 percent. Small independent businesses, such as Healthful Match, Inc., control the final 10 percent, valued at approximately $200 million annually. Healthful Match, Inc., expects to capture one-tenth, or $200,000.
How will you price your products or services? (Describe your proposed pricing structure. Use tables as needed. In this example, the actual tables aren't included).	Sushi, Inc., plans to offer competitive prices for specialty beverages and nigiri sushi as shown in Tables A and B [not shown]. For comparison, Table C [not shown] lists average sushi prices charged by similar establishments in the area. **Note: Provide tables listing specific information for comparison.**
How will you reach the intended target audience to let them know about your products or services? (Describe your advertising plan). **Note: Direct mail marketing and door-to-door distribution are efficient and economical ways to start and build a new customer base.**	Ace Mobile Lube, Inc., plans to initiate an advertising campaign by distributing discount coupons to attract a customer base. Additional proposed advertising consists of: • Contacting fleet owners • Posting signs on the van and on public bulletin boards in the community • Distributing flyers and business cards • Advertising in *The Yellow Pages* and in the service sections of the daily newspapers

	• Offering services on computer bulletin boards Future techniques may include direct mail marketing, door-to-door distribution of flyers, and radio or television commercial advertisements.

Marketing Plan

Ace Mobile Lube, Inc., (Ace) proposes to provide basic automotive services required for the routine maintenance of fleet vehicles, commuter vehicles (capacity up to 18 passengers), vans, smaller commercial trucks (up to 25 feet in length), and privately-owned passenger automobiles or pick-up trucks. Service is available for owners of any vehicle make or model at the location designated by the vehicle's owner, including home, apartment, office, or place of employment. Appointments are scheduled at the convenience of the owner. The service isn't intended, either now or in the future, to provide automotive repairs.

Ace plans to provide service for fleet and individual owners and anticipates that after the first year of business, approximately 50 percent of the work will be derived from fleet service contracts and 50 percent from individual customers. The company will seek additional fleet contracts with the goal of expanding the business by a minimum of 25 percent.

The November 1995-1996 edition of *The Yellow Pages* lists approximately seven mobile oil and lube businesses within the metropolitan areas representing a small number of direct competitors. Ace will be based in Denver and is conveniently located within minutes of major metropolitan roadways. As a mobile business, the relatively close proximity of similar businesses will have little impact on Ace. The company expects to capture approximately 1/8 of the market after the first year in business.

Reasonable prices are charged at a fixed fee rather than on an hourly basis and typical services, sold as packages, are listed in Table A. Other services, such as tire rotation and radiator pressure testing, are available for an additional fixed fee.

Table A—Typical Service Packages

Oil Change & Lube Package $19.95	Basic Package $24.95	
• Change oil (up to 5 quarts) • Replace oil filter	• Change oil (up to 5 quarts) • Replace oil filter • Lubricate chassis • Check differentials • Check and fill tires • Inspect air filter • Inspect wiper blades • Inspect crankcase breather filter	• Clean exterior windows • Vacuum interior • Check brake fluid* • Check power-steering fluid* • Check windshield fluid* • Check battery level* • Check anti-freeze level* • Check automatic transmission fluid*
		*Fill fluids up to 1 pint.

171

Initial advertising includes the distribution of discount coupons to help attract customers. Proposed advertising consists of:

- Directly contacting fleet owners
- Posting signs on the van and on public bulletin boards in the community
- Distributing flyers and business cards
- Advertising in *The Yellow Pages* and in the daily newspapers

Future techniques may include direct-mail marketing, door-to-door distribution of flyers, and radio or television commercial advertisements.

Controlled or protected conditions are required for performance of certain types of service operations. In the future, Ace anticipates either opening a small shop or leasing a service bay where employees can provide specialty services to conditioning systems, transmissions, and radiators. A small shop also provides storage areas for inventory and spent fluids, protected parking for the van, and office space.

Ace has identified areas for possible future expansion of mobile goods and services, such as those listed in Table B. As business increases, a second van and an employee to operate the van may be needed to meet service demand.

Table B—Possible Future Services

Services	
• Provide specialty products, such as engine enhancers and gasoline additives	• Service air conditioners for private passenger vehicles and food-service trucks
• Replace hoses/compressors	• Drain and flush radiators
• Replace worn belts	• Provide tire rotation
• Install oil cooling systems	• Install fuel filters
• Provide road-side assistance	• Provide service for larger trucks (e.g., "18-wheelers")

Table 4.1—Items Relevant to Present and Past Financial History of the Company.

- Year-end balance sheet for last three years[1]
- Year-end profit and loss statement for last three years[1]
- Federal tax returns for the last three years[1]
- Most current interim balance sheet[1]
- Most current interim profit and loss statement[1]
- Current personal financial statement of each owner
- Personal federal tax returns of each owner for last three years
- Cash-flow projection for 12 or 36 months, depending on the situation (36 months is more relevant to a business plan than to a loan or investment request)

Note: (1) In new and start-up business situations, there is no financial history. Therefore, a projected balance sheet and cash-flow statement will satisfy most of the financial history requirements of a loan proposal package.

Table 4.2—Your Balance Sheet Projection for One Month.

Assets		Amount
Current Assets:		
Cash in Bank	$ 17,500	
Accounts Receivable.	5,000	
Inventory	3,000	
Total Current Assets		**$25,500**
Fixed Assets:		
Auto (Delivery Truck)	$10,500	
Less: Depreciation	292	
Net Fixed Assets		**$10,208**
Total Assets		**$35,708**
Liabilities		**Amount**
Current Liabilities:		
Accounts Payable	$ 2,500	
Notes Payable/Line of Credit	2,000	
Total Current Liabilities		**$4,500**
Other Liabilities:		
Note Payable/Auto	5,500	**5,500**
Total Liabilities		**$10,000**
Stockholder's Equity:		
Owner's Draw	$ (2,500)	
Capital Stock	20,000	
Net Profit	8,208	
Total Stockholder's Equity		**$25,708**
Total Liabilities & Stockholder's Equity		**$35,708**

Table 4.3—Example of a 12-month Cash-flow Projection.

MONTHS:	1	2	3	4	5	6	7
CASH AVAILABLE							
Cash on Hand (beginning of month)	—	5,424	16,799	17,299	18,849	19,454	20,120
Net Cash Sales[1]	25,000	26,250	26,250	26,250	26,250	26,250	26,250
Collection of Accounts Receivable.	—	5,000	5,500	6,050	6,655	7,320	8,052
Total Cash Receipts	25,000	31,250	31,750	32,300	32,905	33,570	34,302
Loan/Cash Injections	15,000	—	—	—	—	—	—
Total Cash Available[1]	**40,000**	**31,250**	**31,750**	**32,300**	**32,905**	**33,570**	**34,302**
CASH PAID OUT							
Salaries	6,000	6,000	6,000	6,000	6,000	6,000	6,000
Benefits 12%	720	720	720	720	720	720	720
Lease	800	800	800	800	800	800	800
Utilities	500	500	500	500	500	500	500
Insurance	300	300	300	300	300	300	300
Maintenance & Repairs	50	50	50	50	50	50	50
Telephones	500	500	500	500	500	500	500
Advertising	1,500	1,500	1,500	500	500	500	500
Credit Card Expense	125	125	125	125	125	125	125
Office Supplies	150	150	150	150	150	150	150
SBA Loan Interest	125	—	—	—	—	—	—
Postage	300	300	300	300	300	300	300
Sub Total	**11,070**	**10,945**	**10,945**	**9,945**	**9,945**	**9,945**	**9,945**
OTHER CASH EXPENSES							
Owner's Withdrawal	3,000	3,000	3,000	3,000	3,000	3,000	3,000
Principal Loan Payments	506	506	506	506	506	506	506
Capital Purchases[2]	20,000	—	—	—	—	—	—
Total Cash Paid Out	**34,576**	**14,451**	**14,451**	**13,451**	**13,451**	**13,451**	**13,451**
CASH POSITION							
Monthly Cash Position	**5,424**	**16,799**	**17,299**	**18,849**	**19,454**	**20,119**	**20,851**

Notes: (1) These cash-flow projections are based on achieving annual sales of at least $30,000 per month over the first 12 months. The sales are based on achieving approximately $1,200 per day for five days per week. This estimate is based on your sales experience as a previous manager of an office supply business. (2) These expenditures are $3,500 for computer hardware and software; $11,500 for office furnishings, and $5,000 for a used pick up truck for delivery.

174

Table 4.3—Example of a 12-month Cash-flow Projection con't.

8	9	10	11	12	TOTAL	MONTHS:
						CASH AVAILABLE
20,852	21,657	22,543	23,517	24,589	—	Cash on Hand (beginning of month)
26,250	26,250	26,250	26,250	26,250	$313,750	Net Cash Sales[1]
8,857	9,743	10,717	11,789	12,968	$ 92,651	Collection of Accounts Receivable.
35,107	35,993	36,967	38,039	39,218	$406,401	Total Cash Receipts
—	—	—			$ 15,000	Loan/Cash Injections
35,107	**35,993**	**36,967**	**38,039**	**39,218**	**$421,401**	**Total Cash Available[1]**
						CASH PAID OUT
6,000	6,000	6,000	6,000	6,000	$ 72,000	Salaries
720	720	720	720	720	$ 8,640	Benefits 12%
800	800	800	800	800	$ 9,600	Lease
500	500	500	500	500	$ 6,000	Utilities
300	300	300	300	300	$ 3,600	Insurance
50	50	50	50	50	$ 600	Maintenance & Repairs
500	500	500	500	500	$ 6,000	Telephones
500	500	500	500	500	$ 9,000	Advertising
125	125	125	125	125	$ 1,500	Credit Card Expense
150	150	150	150	150	$ 1,800	Office Supplies
—	—	—	—	—	$ 125	SBA Loan Interest
300	300	300	300	300	$ 3,600	Postage
9,945	**9,945**	**9,945**	**9,945**	**9,945**	**$122,465**	**Subtotal**
						OTHER CASH EXPENSES
3,000	3,000	3,000	3,000	3,000	$ 36,000	Owner's Withdrawal
506	506	506	506	506	$ 6,072	Principal Loan Payments
—	—	—	—	—	$ 20,000	Capital Purchases[2]
13,451	**13,451**	**13,451**	**13,451**	**13,451**	**$184,537**	**Total Cash Paid Out**
						CASH POSITION
21,656	**22,542**	**23,516**	**24,588**	**25,767**	**$236,864**	**Monthly Cash Position**

Notes: (1) These cash-flow projections are based on achieving annual sales of at least $30,000 per month over the first 12 months. The sales are based on achieving approximately $1,200 per day for five days per week. This estimate is based on your sales experience as a previous manager of an office supply business. (2) These expenditures are $3,500 for computer hardware and software; $11,500 for office furnishings, and $5,000 for a used pick up truck for delivery.

Table 4.4—Statement of Profit and Loss for the First 30 Days in Business.

Item	Amount	Subtotal	Total	Percent
Sales			**$30,000**	
Less:				
Merchandise Purchases	$12,000			
Cost of Sales		$12,000	$12,000	(40%)
Gross Profit			**$18,000**	(60%)
Less:				
Operating Expenses:				
Warehouse Salaries	$ 3,350			
Office Supplies (Start-up)	500			
Telephone Set Up	500			
Telephone	250			
Rent	1,500			
Loan Interest	400			
Depreciation	292			
		$10,292		
Total Expenses				
Net Profit			**$8,208**	(27%)

Table 4.5—Typical Information Required for a Personal Financial Statement.

Item	Asset	Liability	Description
Cash on hand & in bank	$ 7,500	—	—
Accounts payable	—	$ 500	Dept. store
Accounts & notes receivable	100	—	Loan to friend
Notes payable to banks and others	—	1,500	Stock purchase
IRA & other retirement accounts	10,500	—	—
Installment account (auto)	—	4,700	$225 per month
Life insurance (cash surrender value)	3,300	—	Face value $100,000
Installment account (other)	—	1,800	Credit cards
Stocks & bonds	10,000	—	Three blue chips
Loans on Life Insurance	—	0	—
Real estate	175,000	—	Residence
Real estate	90,000	—	1/3 share of mountain retreat
Real estate mortgage	—	75,000	ABC Mtg., Denver, CO
Automobile	12,500	—	1995 Pontiac
Unpaid taxes	0	0	—
Other personal property	75,000	—	Jewelry
Other liabilities	—	0	—
Other assets	15,000	—	Stamp collection
Total assets	**$398,900**	—	—
Total liabilities	—	**$ 83,500**	—
Net worth (assets minus liabilities)			**$ 315,400**

Table 5.1—SBA Standard Form 4 (Required Statements).

Introduction
Federal executive agencies, including the Small Business Administration (SBA), are required to withhold or limit financial assistance, to impose special conditions on approved loans, to provide special notices to applicants or borrowers and to require special reports and data from borrowers in order to comply with legislation passed by the Congress and Executive Orders issued by the President and by the provisions of various inter-agency agreements. SBA has issued regulations and procedures that implement these laws and executive orders, and they are contained in Parts 112, 113, 116, and 117, Title 13, Code of Federal Regulations Chapter 1, or Standard Operating Procedures.
Freedom of Information Act (5 U.S.C. 552)
This law provides, with some exceptions, that SBA must supply information reflected in agency files and records to a person requesting it. Information about approved loans that will be automatically released includes, among other things, statistics on our loan programs (individual borrowers are not identified in the statistics) and other information such as the names of the borrowers (and their officers, directors, stockholders or partners), the collateral pledged to secure the loan, the amount of the loan, its purpose in general terms and the maturity. Proprietary data on a borrower would not routinely be made available to third parties. All requests under this Act are to be addressed to the nearest SBA office and be identified as a Freedom of Information request.
Right to Financial Privacy Act of 1978 (12 U.S.C. 3401)
This is notice to you as required by the Right to Financial Privacy Act of 1978, of SBA's access rights to financial records held by financial institutions that are or have been doing business with you or your business, including any financial institutions participating in a loan or loan guarantee. The law provides that SBA shall have a right of access to your financial records in connection with its consideration or administration of assistance to you in the form of a Government loan or loan guaranty agreement. SBA is required to provide a certificate of its compliance with the Act to a financial institution in connection with its first request for access to your financial records, after which no further certification is required for subsequent accesses. The law also provides that SBA's access rights continue for the term of any approved loan or loan guaranty agreement. No further notice to you of SBA's access rights is required during the term of any such agreement. The law also authorizes SBA to transfer to another Government authority any financial records included in an application for a loan, or concerning an approved loan or loan guarantee, as necessary to process, service or foreclose on a loan or loan guarantee or to collect on a defaulted loan or loan guarantee. No other transfer of your financial records to another Government authority will be permitted by SBA except as required or permitted by law.
Flood Disaster Protection Act (42 U.S.C. 4011)
Regulations have been issued by the Federal Insurance Administration (FIA) and by SBA implementing this Act and its amendments. These regulations prohibit SBA from making certain loans in an FIA designated floodplain unless Federal flood insurance is purchased as a condition of the loan. Failure to maintain the required level of flood insurance makes the applicant ineligible for any future financial assistance from SBA under any program, including disaster assistance.
Executive Orders—Floodplain Management and Wetland Protection (42 F. R. 26951 and 42 F.R. 26961)
The SBA discourages any settlement in or development of a floodplain or a wetland. This statement is to notify all SBA loan applicants that such actions are hazardous to both life and property and should be avoided. The additional cost of flood preventive construction must be considered in addition to the possible loss of all assets and investments in future floods.

Occupational Safety and Health Act (15 U.S.C. 651 et seq.)

This legislation authorizes the Occupational Safety and Health Administration in the Department of Labor to require businesses to modify facilities and procedures to protect employees or pay penalty fees. In some instances the business can be forced to cease operations or be prevented from starting operations in a new facility. Therefore, in some instances SBA may require additional information from an applicant to determine whether the business will be in compliance with OSHA regulations and allowed to operate its facility after the loan is approved and disbursed.

Signing this form as borrower is a certification that the OSHA requirements that apply to the borrower's business have been determined and the borrower to the best of its knowledge is in compliance.

Civil Rights Legislation

All businesses receiving SBA financial assistance must agree not to discriminate in any business practice, including employment practices and services to the public, on the basis of categories cited in 13 C.F.R., Parts 112, 113 and 117 of SBA Regulations. This includes making their goods and services available to handicapped clients or customers. All business borrowers will be required to display the "Equal Employment Opportunity Poster" prescribed by SBA.

Equal Credit Opportunity Act (15 U.S.C. 1691)

The Federal Equal Credit Opportunity Act prohibits creditors from discriminating against credit applicants on the basis of race, color, religion, national origin, sex, marital status or age (provided that the applicant has the capacity to enter into a binding contract), because all or part of the applicant's income derives from any public assistance program, or because the applicant has in good faith exercised any right under the Consumer Credit Protection Act. The Federal agency that administers compliance with this law concerning this creditor is the Federal Trade Commission, Equal Credit Opportunity, Washington, D.C., 20580.

Executive Order 11738—Environmental Protection (38 F. R. 25161)

The Executive Order charges SBA with administering its loan programs in a manner that will result in effective enforcement of the Clean Air Act, the Federal Water Pollution Act and other environmental protection legislation. SBA must, therefore, impose conditions on some loans. By acknowledging receipt of this form and presenting the application, the principals of all small businesses borrowing $100,000 or more in direct funds stipulate to the following:

1. That any facility used, or to be used, by the subject firm is not cited on the EPA list of Violating Facilities.
2. That subject firm will comply with all the requirements of Section 114 of the Clean Air Act (42 U.S.C. 7414) and Section 308 of the Water Act (33 U.S.C. 1318) relating to inspection, monitoring, entry, reports and information, as well as all other requirements specified in Section 114 and Section 308 of the respective Acts, and all regulations and guidelines issued thereunder.
3. That subject firm will notify SBA of the receipt of any communication from the Director of the Environmental Protection Agency indicating that a facility utilized, or to be utilized, by subject firm is under consideration to be listed on the EPA List of Violating Facilities.

Debt Collection Act of 1982 Deficit Reduction Act of 1984
(31 U.S. C. 3701 et seq. and other titles)

These laws require SBA to aggressively collect any loan payments which become delinquent. SBA must obtain your taxpayer identification number when you apply for a loan. If you receive a loan, and do not make payments as they come due, SBA may take one or more of the following actions:

- Report the status of your loan(s) to credit bureaus
- Hire a collection agency to collect your loan
- Offset your income tax refund or other amounts due to you from the Federal Government
- Suspend or debar you or your company from doing business with the Federal Government
- Refer your loan to the Department of Justice or other attorneys for litigation
- Foreclose on collateral or take other action permitted in the loan instruments.

Immigration Reform and Control Act of 1986 (Pub. L. 99-603)

If you are an alien who was in this country illegally since before January 1, 1982, you may have been granted lawful temporary resident status by the United States Immigration and Naturalization Service pursuant to the Immigration Reform and Control Act of 1986 (Pub. L. 99-603). For five years from the date you are granted such status, you are not eligible for financial assistance from the SBA in the form of a loan or guaranty under section 7(a) of the Small Business Act unless you are disabled or a Cuban or Haitian entrant. When you sign this document, you are making the certification that the Immigration Reform and Control Act of 1986 does not apply to you, or if it does apply, more than five years have elapsed since you have been granted lawful temporary resident status pursuant to such 1986 legislation.

Lead-based Paint Poisoning Prevention Act (42 U.S.C. 4821 et seq.)

Borrowers using SBA funds for the construction or rehabilitation of a residential structure are prohibited from using lead-based paint (as defined in SBA regulations) on all interior surfaces, whether accessible or not, and exterior surfaces, such as stairs, decks, porches, railings, windows and doors, which are readily accessible to children under 7 years of age. A "residential structure" is any home, apartment, hotel, motel, orphanage, boarding school, dormitory, day care center, extended care facility, college or other school housing, hospital, group practice or community facility and all other residential or institutional structures where persons reside.

Table 5.11—SBA Standard Form 159 (Policy and Regulations Concerning Representatives and their Fees)

Item	Comment
An applicant for a loan from SBA may obtain the assistance of any attorney, accountant, engineer, appraiser or other representative to aid him in the preparation and presentation of his application to SBA; however, such representation is not mandatory. In the event a loan is approved, the services of an attorney may be necessary to assist in the preparation of closing documents, title abstracts, etc. SBA will allow the payment of reasonable fees or other compensation for services performed by such representatives on behalf of the applicant.	If you find that you need the help of an attorney, accountant, engineer, appraiser or other professional, the SBA allows you to hire these services for a reasonable fee, although assistance from these professionals is not mandatory and is left to your discretion.
There are no "authorized representatives" of SBA, other than our regular salaried employees. Payment of any fee or gratuity to SBA employees is illegal and will subject the parties to such a transaction to prosecution.	Be wary of any professional who suggests that they are authorized SBA representatives. SBA has no authorized representatives. SBA also prohibits any type of payment ("bribe") to SBA employees.
SBA Regulations (Part 103, Sec. 103.13-5(c)) prohibit representatives from charging or proposing to charge any contingent fee for any services performed in connection with an SBA loan unless the amount of such fee bears a necessary and reasonable relationship to the services actually performed; or to charge for any expenses which are not deemed by SBA to have been necessary in connection with the application. The Regulations (Part 120, Sec. 120.104-2) also prohibit the payment of any bonus, brokerage fee or commission in connection with SBA loans.	If you have a professional or consultant working with you in obtaining your SBA loan, payment is subject to SBA regulations. These regulations also prohibit the payment of bonuses, brokerage fees, or commissions.
In line with these Regulations SBA will not approve placement or finder's fees for the use or attempted use of influence in obtaining or trying to obtain an SBA loan, or fees based solely upon a percentage of the approved loan or any part thereof.	Avoid any professional or consultant who suggests to you that they want as payment a cut from any loan amount you receive.
Fees which will be approved will be limited to reasonable sums of services actually rendered in connection with the application or the closing, based upon the time and effort required, the qualifications of the representative and the nature and extent of the services rendered by such representatives. Representatives of loan applicants will be required to execute an	SBA wants to assure that any representative that you work with charges reasonable fees appropriately relevant to their services.

agreement as to their compensation for services rendered in connection with said loan.	
It is the responsibility of the applicant to set forth in the appropriate section of the application the names of all persons or firms engaged by or on behalf of the applicant. Applicants are required to advise the Regional Office in writing the names and fees of any representatives engaged by the applicant subsequent to the filing of the application. This reporting requirement is approved under OMB Approval Number 2345-0016.	Provide the SBA with the names of either professionals, consultants, or other persons who are engaged on your behalf to obtain an SBA loan.
Any loan applicant having any question concerning the payments of fees, or the reasonableness of fees, should communicate with the Field Office where the application is filed.	If you are not sure that you are being charged reasonable fees, contact you SBA Field Office.

Table 5.12—SBA Standard Form 159 (Instructions Policy and Regulations Concerning Representatives and their Fees)

Item	Comment
The undersigned representative (attorney, accountant, engineer, appraiser, etc.) hereby agrees that the undersigned has not and will not, directly or indirectly, charge or receive any payment in connection with the application for or the making of the loan except for services actually performed on behalf of the Applicant. The undersigned further agrees that the amount of payment for such services shall not exceed an amount deemed reasonable by SBA (and, if it is a participation loan, by the participating lending institution), and to refund any amount in excess of that deemed reasonable by SBA (and the participating institution). This agreement shall supersede any other agreement covering payment for such services.	The professional or consultant certifies by signing that the fees have been reasonable.
A general description of the services performed, or to be performed, by the undersigned and the compensation paid or to be paid are set forth below. **If the total compensation in any case exceeds $1,000 (or $300 for: (1) regular business loans of $15,000 or less; or (2) all disaster home loans) or if SBA should otherwise require, the services must be itemized on a schedule attached showing each date services were performed, time spent each day, and description of service rendered on each day listed.**	If the professional's costs for services exceed $1,000, then each service must be itemized and broken down by dates into descriptions of the services and the associated costs for each.
The undersigned Applicant and representative hereby certify that no other fees have been charged or will be charged by the representative in connection with this loan, unless provided for in the loan authorization specifically approved by SBA.	Read this information.

GENERAL DESCRIPTION OF SERVICES
    Paid Previously $_____
    Additional Amount to be Paid $_____
    Total Compensation $_____
	Provide this information. The information must coincide with SBA's compensation guidelines.

(Section 13 of the Small Business Act (15 USC 642) requires disclosures concerning fees. Parts 103, 108 and 120 of Title 13 of the Code of Federal Regulations contain provisions covering appearances and compensation of persons representing SBA applicants. Section 103.13-5 authorizes the suspension or revocation of the	Read this information.

privilege of any such person to appear before SBA for charging a fee deemed unreasonable by SBA for services actually performed, charging of unreasonable expenses, or violation of this agreement. Whoever commits any fraud, by false or misleading statement or representation, or by conspiracy, shall be subject to the penalty of any applicable Federal or State statute.)	
Dated_____, _____ _____ (Representative) By_____	Provide this information.
The Applicant hereby certifies to SBA that the above representations, description of services, and amounts are correct and satisfactory to Applicant.	Read this information.
Dated_____, _____ _____ (Applicant) By_____	Provide this information.
The participating lending institution hereby certifies that the above representations of service rendered and amounts charged are reasonable and satisfactory to it.	Read this information.
Dated_____, _____ _____ (Lender) By_____	Provide this information.
NOTE: Foregoing certification must be executed, if by a corporation, in corporate name by duly authorized officer and duly attested; if by a partnership, in the firm name, together with signature of a general partner.	Read this information.

Table 5.2—SBA Standard Form 4, Page 1, Lines 1 through 6 (Basic Business Information).

For You as an Individual:	
Item	**Comment**
Individual.	Use your full legal name
Full Address.	Use your personal address.
For Your Business:	
Item	**Comment**
Name of Applicant Business.	Use the full legal name of your business.
Full Street Address of Business.	Use the full street address of your business.
City, County, State, and Zip.	Enter this information for the applicant business.
Tax ID No. or SSN.	Use either your FEIN or your Social Security number, if you're a sole proprietor.
Tel. No. (inc. A/C).	Use your business telephone number, beginning with the area code.
Number of Employees (including subsidiaries and affiliates): • At Time of Loan Application. • If Loan is Approved. • Subsidiaries or Affiliates (Separate from above).	Enter the appropriate number: • If you don't plan to add employees immediately after the loan is approved, then the number of employees will be the same for the first two items; and • Indicate the number of employees you have at locations other than your primary location at the time of application.
Type of Business.	Identify your business type and refer to the appropriate SIC.
Date Business Established.	Enter the date your business was established. This will depend upon the legal structure of your business (for a sole proprietorship use the date you first started doing business; for a partnership use the date your agreement was signed; for a corporation, use the date of incorporation).
Bank of Business Account and Address.	List your bank's name and the full street address.

Table 5.3—SBA Standard Form 4, Page 1, Lines 7 through 13 (Use of Proceeds).

Land Acquisition.	Enter the purchase value of any land that you're planning to buy for use in the operation of your business and be prepared to demonstrate why the purchase is more advantageous than a lease.
New Construction/ Expansion/ Repair.	Enter the amount that will be used for either new construction or expansion and/or repair of any building you're considering. Be prepared to demonstrate that you have solicited bids from several contractors and that you have checked their references.
Acquisition and/or Repair of Machinery and Equipment.	Enter the amount that will be used for either the purchase or repair of capital equipment and be prepared to demonstrate that you have written quotes from vendors.
Inventory Purchase.	Enter the amount you'll need to establish an inventory necessary to transact business.
Working Capital (including Accounts Payable).	Enter the amount you'll need as working capital for day-to-day business expenses and refer to your profit and loss and monthly cash-flow projections as a guideline in developing an appropriate amount.
Acquisition of Existing Business.	Since this is a business start-up, don't enter an amount here—indicate "n/a."
Payoff SBA Loan.	Since this is a business start-up, this may not be relevant—indicate "n/a," if appropriate.
Payoff Bank Loan (Non SBA Associated).	Enter the amount that will be applied to an existing bank loan that isn't associated with an SBA loan.
Other Debt Payment (Non SBA Associated).	Enter the amount that will be applied to any other debt payment that isn't associated with an SBA loan.
All Other.	Enter any other amounts that are relevant and attach a list of items and amounts, such as unplanned expenses, or contingencies, that may be valued from 5 to 20 percent of the loan amount.
Total Loan Requested.	Enter the amount of the total loan requested and assure that the amount is equal to the sum of the amounts listed in this section.
Term of Loan (Requested Mat.).	Enter the total number of months or years you want the loan to cover, usually 5 to 7 years for working capital loans with a maximum of 25 years for a real estate purchase.

Table 5.4—SBA Standard Form 4 Page 2 (Management).

Item	Comment
Name and Social Security number and Position Title.	Provide this information for the business' primary owners/officers (list the owners in the order of their importance).
Complete Address.	Provide residential street addresses.
% Owned.	Show 100% ownership (this is required).
*Military Service [Dates] From and To.	Provide this information for statistical purposes—this information has no bearing on credit decisions associated with your application.
*Race.	Provide this information for statistical purposes—this information has no bearing on credit decisions associated with your application.
*Sex.	Provide this information for statistical purposes—this information has no bearing on credit decisions associated with your application.
*This data is collected for statistical purposes only. It has no bearing on the credit decision to approve or decline this application.	

Table 5.5—SBA Standard Form 4 Pages 2 and 3 (Exhibits).

Introduction	Comments
For Guaranty Loans please provide an original and one copy (photocopy is acceptable) of the Application Form, and all Exhibits to the participating lender. For Direct Loans submit one original copy of the application and Exhibits to SBA.	Be sure to make one or more copies for your records (see Chapter 7—Compiling Your Loan Proposal Package). Note that Direct Loans are no longer available.
1. Submit SBA Form 912 (Personal History Statement) for each person e.g. owners, partners, officers, directors, major stockholders, etc.; the instructions are on SBA Form 912.	Be attentive to questions regarding arrest and conviction (arrest for traffic violations must be included).
2. If your collateral consists of: (A) Land and Building, (B) Machinery and Equipment, (C) Furniture and Fixtures, (D) Accounts Receivable, . (E) Inventory, (F) Other, Please provide an itemized list (labeled **Exhibit A**) that contains serial and identification numbers for all articles that had an original value greater than $500. Include a legal description of Real Estate offered as collateral.	Provide information on collateral. Refer to the discussion of SBA Standard Form 4 Schedule A—Schedule of Collateral, Exhibit A, included in this chapter.
3. Furnish a signed current personal balance sheet (SBA Form 413 may be used for this purpose) for each stockholder (with 20% or greater ownership), partner, officer, and owner. Social Security number should be included on personal financial statement. It should be as of the same date as the most recent business financial statements. Label this **Exhibit B**.	Provide a personal balance sheet.

4.	Include the statements listed below: 1, 2, 3 for the last three years; also 1, 2, 3, 4 as of the same date, which are current within 90 days of filing the application; and statement 5, if applicable. This is **Exhibit C** (SBA has Management Aids that help in the preparation of financial statements). All information must be **signed and dated**. 1. Balance Sheet 2. Profit and Loss Statement 3. Reconciliation of Net Worth 4. Aging of Accounts Receivable .and Payable. 5. Earnings projected for at least one year where financial statements for the last three years are unavailable or where requested by District Office. (If Profit and Loss Statement is not available, explain why and substitute Federal Income Tax Forms).	None of these items are applicable to start-up businesses. Note that Exhibit C is also part of a business plan and is discussed in Chapter 4 (Understanding Financial Matters).
5.	Provide a brief history of your company and a paragraph describing the expected benefits it will receive from the loan. Label it **Exhibit D**.	For a business start-up, your discussion may be limited to your concept.
6.	Provide a brief description similar to a resume of the education, technical and business background for all the people listed under Management. Please mark it **Exhibit E**.	Use your current resume or prepare one.
7.	Do you have any co-signers and/or guarantors for this loan? If so, please submit their names, addresses, Tax ID Numbers, and current personal balance sheet(s) as **Exhibit F**.	See Chapter 4 (Understanding Financial Matters).
8.	Are you buying machinery or equipment with your loan money? If so, you must include a list of equipment and cost as quoted by the seller and his name and address. This is **Exhibit G**.	Provide an itemized list of machinery or equipment that you plan to purchase with the proceeds. This information can also be presented on the schedule of collateral (SBA Standard Form 4 ,, Schedule A).
9.	Have you or any officer of your company ever been involved in bankruptcy or insolvency proceedings? If so, please provide the details as **Exhibit H**. If none, check here: Yes or No	Provide details if either you or any company officer has been involved in bankruptcy or insolvency proceedings.

10	Are you or your business involved in any pending lawsuits? If yes, provide the details as **Exhibit I**. If none, check here: Yes or No	Provide details if either you or any company officer is involved in any unresolved lawsuits.
11.	Do you or your spouse or any member of your household, or anyone who owns, manages, or directs your business or their spouses or members of their households work for the Small Business Administration, Small Business Advisory Council, SCORE or ACE, any Federal Agency, or the participating lender? If so, please provide the name and address of the person and the office where employed. Label this **Exhibit J**. If none, check here: Yes or No	Read and answer if needed. You need only provide Exhibit J if you have relevant information—otherwise, check "No."
12.	Does your business, its owners or majority stockholders own or have a controlling interest in other businesses? If yes, please provide their names and the relationship with your company along with a current balance sheet and operating statement for each. This should be **Exhibit K**.	Provide information regarding any affiliates or subsidiaries, including financial statements for each.
13.	Do you buy from, sell to, or use the services of any concern in which someone in your company has a significant financial interest? If yes, provide details on a separate sheet of paper labeled **Exhibit L**.	If anyone in your company has a significant financial interest in another company that you plan to transact business with, provide the details.
14.	If your business is a franchise, include a copy of the franchise agreement and a copy of the FTC disclosure statement supplied to you by the Franchiser. Please include it as Exhibit M.	Provide a copy of any relevant franchise agreement. You need only provide Exhibit M if you have relevant information.
Construction Loans Only		**Comment**
15.	Include a separate exhibit (**Exhibit N**) the estimated cost of the project and a statement of the source of any additional funds.	Provide this information if you're using loan proceeds for construction.
16.	Provide copies of preliminary construction plans and specifications. Include them as **Exhibit O**. Final plans will be required prior to disbursement.	Provide this information if you're using loan proceeds for construction.

Direct Loans Only	Comment
17. Include two bank declination letters with your application. (In cities with 200,000 people or less, one letter will be sufficient). These letters should include the name and telephone number of the persons contacted at the banks, the amount and terms of the loan, the reason for decline and whether or not the bank will participate with SBA.	No longer available.
Export Loans	**Comment**
18. Does your business presently engage in Export Trade? Check here: Yes or No	Answer yes or no.
19. Do you have plans to begin exporting as a result of this loan? Check here: Yes or No	Answer yes or no.
20. Would you like information on Exporting? Check here: Yes or No	Answer yes or no.
Agreements and Certifications	**Comment**
Agreements of non-employment of SBA Personnel: I agree that if SBA approves this loan application I will not, for at least two years, hire as an employee or consultant anyone that was employed by the SBA during the one year period prior to the disbursement of the loan.	Read the agreements and certifications because your signature indicates that you'll comply with the appropriate government regulations.

Certification: I certify:	Read this information.
(a) I have not paid anyone connected with the Federal Government for help in getting this loan. I also agree to report to the SBA office of the Inspector General, Washington, D.C., 20416, any Federal Government employee who offers, in return for any type of compensation, to help get this loan approved.	
(b) All information in this application and the Exhibits are true and complete to the best of my knowledge and are submitted to SBA so SBA can decide whether to grant a loan or participate with a lending institution in a loan to me. I agree to pay for or reimburse SBA for the cost of any surveys, title or mortgage examinations, appraisals, credit reports, etc., performed by non-SBA personnel provided I have given my consent.	
(c) I understand that I need not pay anybody to deal with SBA. I have read and understand SBA Form 159— which explains SBA policy on representatives and their fees.	
(d) As consideration for any Management, Technical, and Business Development Assistance that may be provided, I waive all claims against SBA and its consultants.	
If you make a statement that you know to be false or if you over value a security in order to help obtain a loan under the provisions of the Small Business Act, you can be fined up to $5,000 or be put in jail for up to two years, or both.	Read this information.

Most of the items on this form are numbered, however some aren't. Information requested by this form is itemized in Table 5.6 in the order in which each item appears on the form.

Table 5.6—SBA Standard Form 912 (Statement of Personal History).

Item	Comment
Name and Address of Applicant. (Firm Name) (Street, City, State, and ZIP Code)	Enter your company's name and address (or your home address if you don't have a location for your business yet).
SBA District/Disaster Area Office.	Enter the appropriate information for the SBA location where you are applying.
Amount Applied for (when applicable):	Enter the loan amount requested (this should agree with the amount shown on SBA Standard Form 4).
File No. (if known).	Leave this blank—the SBA office will fill in the appropriate information.
Name and Address of participating bank, lender, or surety company (when applicable and known).	Enter the information for the bank, lender, or surety company.
1. Personal Statement of: (State name in full, if no middle name, state (NMN), or if initial only, indicate initial). List all former names used, and dates each name was used. Use separate sheet if necessary. First Middle Last	Enter the full legal name of the person whose personal history is presented on the form and include former names and dates of use.
2. Date of Birth: (Month, day, and year).	Enter the birth date of the person whose personal history is presented on the form.
3. Place of Birth: (City & State or Foreign Country).	Enter the place of birth of the person whose personal history is presented on the form.
4. Give the percentage of ownership or stock owned or to be owned in the small business concern or the Development Company.	Enter the percentage of ownership or stock owned by the person whose personal history is presented on the form.
Social Security No.	Enter the Social Security number of the person whose personal history is presented on the form.
U.S. Citizen? Yes or No If no, give the alien registration number:	Select either "yes" or "no"—if "no," give the alien registration number.

5. Present residence address: From: To: Address: Home Telephone No. (Include A/C): Business Telephone No. (Include A/C): Most recent prior address (omit if over 10 years ago): From: To: Address:	It's important to present exact information and dates regarding present and prior addresses.
It is against SBA's policy to provide assistance to persons not of good character; therefore, consideration is given to a person's behavior, integrity, candor, and disposition toward criminal actions. It is also against SBA's policy to provide assistance not in the best interest of the United States; for example, if there is reason to believe the effect of such assistance will be to encourage or support, directly or indirectly, activities inimical to the security of the United States.	Read this information.
Therefore, it is important that the next three questions be answered truthfully and completely. An arrest or conviction record will not necessarily disqualify you; however, an untruthful answer will cause your application to be denied.	Read this information.
The fact that you have an arrest or conviction record will not necessarily disqualify you. But an incorrect answer will probably cause your application to be turned down.	Read this information.
If you answer "yes" to 6, 7, or 8, furnish details in a separate exhibit. Include dates, location, fines, sentences, whether misdemeanor or felony, dates of parole/probation; unpaid fines or penalties; name(s) under which charged, and any other pertinent information.	Read this information and provide the requested details, if appropriate.
6. Are you presently under indictment, on parole or probation? Yes or No (If yes, indicate date parole or probation is to expire.)	Select either "yes" or "no"—if "yes" provide the requested information.
10. Have you ever been charged with or arrested for any criminal offense other than a minor motor vehicle violation? Include offenses which have been dismissed, discharged, or nolle prosequi. (All arrests and charges must be disclosed and explained on an attached sheet). Yes or No	Select either "yes" or "no"—if "yes" provide the requested information.

8.	Have you <u>ever</u> been convicted, placed on pretrial diversion, or placed on any form of probation, including adjudication withheld pending probation, for any criminal offense other than a minor motor vehicle violation? Yes or No	Select either "yes" or "no."
9.	I authorize the Small Business Administration Office of Inspector General to request criminal record information about me from criminal justice agencies for the purpose of determining my eligibility for programs authorized by the Small Business Act, as amended.	Read this information.
Caution: Knowingly making a false statement on this form is a violation of Federal law and could result in criminal prosecution, significant civil penalties, and a denial of your loan, surety bond, or other program participation. A false statement is punishable under 18 U.S.C. 1001 by imprisonment of not more than five years and/or a fine of not more than $10,000; under 15 U.S.C. 645 by imprisonment of not more than two years and/or a fine of not more than $5,000; and, if submitted to a Federally insured institution, under 18 U.S.C. 1014 by imprisonment of not more than twenty years and/or a fine of not more than $1,000,000.		Read this information.
Signature, Title, Date		Sign the form, giving your title and the date.
10.	Fingerprints Waived, Date, Approving Authority Fingerprints Required, Date, Approving Authority, Date Sent to OIG	Leave this blank—the SBA office will fill in the appropriate information.
11.	Cleared for Processing, Date, Approving Authority; Request a Character Evaluation, Date, Approving Authority.	Leave this blank—the SBA office will fill in the appropriate information.

Table 5.7—SBA Standard Form 4 Schedule A (Schedule of Collateral, Exhibit A).

Identification	
Item	**Comment**
Applicant.	Provide the name of the business.
Street Address.	Provide the street address of the business.
City, State, and Zip Code.	Provide the city, state and zip code for the business.
LIST ALL COLLATERAL TO BE USED AS SECURITY FOR THIS LOAN.	Follow this instruction.
Section I—Real Estate	
Item	**Comment**
Attach a copy of the deed(s) containing a full legal description of the land and show the location (street address) and city where the deed(s) is recorded. Following the address below, give a brief description of the improvements, such as size, type of construction, use, number of stories, and present condition (use additional sheets if more space is required).	Read this material and follow the instructions.
LIST PARCELS OF REAL ESTATE.	List land and buildings (if you number each of these entries, you can refer to each one by its number when you enter the descriptions below).
• Address	Enter full street address of the parcel.
• Year acquired	Enter the year you acquired the parcel.
• Original cost	Enter the original cost of the parcel.
• Market value	Enter the market value of the parcel.
• Amount of lien	Enter the amount of lien of the parcel, if applicable.
• Name of lienholder	Enter the name of the lienholder, if applicable.
Description(s).	Refer to the entries by number and provide descriptions of each listed parcel (i.e., "two-story brick and frame residential building with 2,000 square feet of space and detached garage"; "_-acre undeveloped commercial lot").
Section II—Personal Property	
Item	**Comment**
All items herein must show manufacturer or make, model, year, and serial number. Items with no serial number must be clearly identified (use additional sheets if more space is required).	Read these instructions.
Description—Show Manufacturer, Model, Serial No.	Provide a clear description of each item.
• Year acquired	Enter year acquired for each item.
• Original cost	Enter the original cost for each item.
• Market value	Enter the current market value for each item.

• Current lien balance	Enter the current lien balance for each item, if applicable.
• Name of lienholder	Enter the name of the lienholder for each item, if applicable.

Signature	
Item	**Comment**
All information contained herein is TRUE and CORRECT to the best of my knowledge. I understand that FALSE statements may result in forfeiture of benefits and possible fine and prosecution by the U.S. Attorney General (Ref. 18 U.S.C. 100).	Read this information.
Signature and Date.	Sign and date the form.

Table 5.8—SBA Standard Form 413 (Personal Financial Statement).

Item	Comment
As of , ,	Enter the date when you completed the application.
Complete this form for: (1) each proprietor, or (2) each limited partner who owns 20% or more interest and each general partner, or (3) each stockholder owning 20% or more of voting stock, or (4) any person or entity providing a guaranty on the loan.	Read this information and following the instructions, as applicable.
Name Business Phone ( )	Enter your name and business or day-time phone number. Include your area code.
Residence Address Residence Phone ( )	Enter your residential street address and home or evening phone number. Include your area code.
City, State, & Zip Code	Enter your city, state, and zip code.
Business Name of Applicant/Borrower	Enter the formal name you use when you sign a legal or business document.
Assets	**Comment (List the amount, as applicable, and omit cents).**
Cash on Hand & in Banks	List cash on hand and in the bank.
Savings Accounts	List every savings account.
IRA or Other Retirement Account	List your retirement accounts.
Accounts & Notes Receivable	List your receivables, if applicable.
Life Insurance—Cash Surrender Value Only (Complete Section 8)	Give details in Section 8. Attach an addendum to the section, if needed. Remember that cash surrender value is **not** the same as the face value of the policy.
Stocks and Bonds (Described in Section 3)	Give details in Section 3 and attach an addendum to the section, if needed.
Real Estate (Described in Section 4)	Give details in Section 4 and attach an addendum to the section, if needed.
Automobile—Present Value	List the present value of your personal vehicles.
Other Personal Property (Described in Section 5)	Give details in Section 5 and attach an addendum to the section, if needed.
Other Assets (Described in Section 5)	Give details in Section 5 and attach an addendum to the section, if needed.
Total	Calculate a total of these amounts.
Liabilities	**Comment (List the amount, as applicable, and omit cents).**
Accounts Payable	List your accounts payable.
Notes Payable to Banks and Others (Described in Section 2)	Give details in Section 2 and attach an addendum to the section, if needed.
Installment Account (Auto) Mo. Payments	List any installment payments for your personal vehicles.
Installment Account (other) Mo. Payments	List any other installment payments you owe.

Loan on Life Insurance	List any loan you may have on your life insurance.
Mortgages on Real Estate (Described in Section 4)	Give details in Section 4 and attach an addendum to the section, if needed.
Unpaid Taxes (Described in Section 6)	Give details in Section 6 and attach an addendum to the section, if needed.
Other Liabilities (Described in Section 7)	Give details in Section 7 and attach an addendum to the section, if needed.
Total Liabilities	Calculate a total of these amounts.
Net Worth	Determine your net worth by subtracting "Total Liabilities" calculated in this section from the "Total" calculated above under "Assets."
Total	Calculate a total by adding "Total Liabilities" and "Net Worth" (this figure should be equal to "Total" calculated above under "Assets").
Section 1. Source of Income	**Comment (List the amount, as applicable, and omit cents).**
Salary	List your salary, if applicable.
Net Investment Income	List your net investment income.
Real Estate Income	List your real estate income.
Other Income (Described below*)	List any other income and provide the details.
*Alimony or child support payments need not be disclosed in "Other Income" unless it is desired to have such payments counted toward total income.	Read this information.
Contingent Liabilities	**Comment (List the amount, as applicable, and omit cents).**
As Endorser or Co-Maker	List any loans you have endorsed or co-signed.
Legal Claims & Judgments	List any legal claims or judgments against you and any that are pending.
Provision for Federal Income Tax	List any liabilities associated with federal income tax.
Other Special Debt	List any other special debt.
Description of Other Income in Section 1	Use this space to describe other income information relevant to this section.
Section 2. Notes Payable to Bank and Others (Use attachments if necessary. Each attachment must be identified as a part of this statement and signed.).	**Comment (List the amount, as applicable, and omit cents. Include the requested information of each note payable).**
Name and Address of Noteholder(s)	Provide the name and address of any noteholder.
Original Balance	List the original balance of the note.
Current Balance	List the current balance of the note.
Payment Amount	List the payment amount of the note.
Frequency (monthly, etc.)	List the frequency of the note payments.
How Secured or Endorsed, Type of Collateral	Describe how the note is secured or what collateral was offered.

Section 3. Stocks and Bonds. (Use attachments if necessary. Each attachment must be identified as a part of this statement and signed).	Comment (List the amount, as applicable, and omit cents. Include this information for each stock and bond).
Number of Shares	List the number of shares you own.
Name of Securities	List the name of each security.
Cost	List the cost of each security.
Market value, Quotation/Exchange	List the market value and quotation and/or exchange for each security.
Date of Quotation/Exchange	Provide the date of the quotation and/or exchange for each security.
Total Value	Calculate the total value for each security you own.
Section 4. Real Estate Owned (List each parcel separately. Use attachments if necessary. Each attachment must be identified as a part of this statement and signed).	Comment (List the amount, as applicable, and omit cents. Complete this information for each property (i.e., Property A, Property B).).
Type of Property	Describe the type of property you own (i.e., residential, commercial, condominiums, time share).
Address	Provide the address.
Date Purchased	Provide the date of purchase.
Original Cost	Provide the original cost.
Present Market Value	Provide the present market value.
Name & Address of Mortgage Holder	Provide the name and address of the mortgage holder.
Mortgage Account Number	Provide the mortgage account number.
Mortgage Balance	Provide the mortgage balance.
Amount of Payment per Month/Year	Provide the amount of payment either per month or per year.
Status of Mortgage	Provide the status of the mortgage (are your payments current or past due?).
Section 5. Other Personal Property and Other Assets. (Describe, and if any is pledged as security, state name and address of lienholder, amount of lien, terms of payment, and if delinquent, describe delinquency).	Comment (List the amount, as applicable, and omit cents).
[blank line]	Use this space to provide information regarding other personal property and assets and include pertinent information.
Section 6. Unpaid Taxes. (Describe in detail, as to type, to whom payable, when due, amount, and to what property, if any, a tax lien attaches).	Comment (List the amount, as applicable, and omit cents).

[blank line]	Use this space to provide information regarding unpaid taxes and include pertinent information such as the type of tax, who you owe, due date, amount, and status of lien.
Section 7. Other Liabilities. (Described in detail).	**Comment (List the amount, as applicable, and omit cents).**
[blank line]	Use this space to provide information about other liabilities and include pertinent information such as the name and address of the person or organization you owe, and the conditions of the liability.
Section 8. Life Insurance Held. (Give face amount and cash surrender value of policies—name of insurance company and beneficiaries).	**Comment (List the amount, as applicable, and omit cents).**
[blank line]	Use this space to provide information regarding your life insurance and include pertinent information such as the name of the insurance company for each policy, the beneficiary, the face amount, and surrender value.
I authorize SBA/Lender to make inquiries as necessary to verify the accuracy of the statements made and to determine my creditworthiness. I certify the above and the statements contained in the attachments are true and accurate as of the stated date(s). These statements are made for the purpose of either obtaining a loan or guaranteeing a loan. I understand FALSE statements may result in forfeiture of benefits and possible prosecution by the U.S. Attorney General (Reference 18 U.S.C. 1001).	Read this information.
Signature: Date: Social Security Number:	Sign and date this form and include your Social Security number.

200

Table 5.9—SBA Standard Form 1624 (Certification Regarding Debarment, Suspension, Ineligibility and Voluntary Exclusion Lower Tier Covered Transactions Instructions).

	Item	Comment
1.	By signing and submitting this proposal, the prospective lower tier participant is providing the certification set out below.	Your are certifying that you and your company have never been barred from doing business with the government.
2.	The certification in this clause is a material representation of fact upon which reliance was placed when this transaction was entered into. If it is later determined that the prospective lower tier participant knowingly rendered an erroneous certification, in addition to other remedies available to the Federal Government, the department or agency with which this transaction originated may pursue available remedies, including suspension and/or debarment.	The federal government relies heavily on your honesty that you have never been debarred.
3.	The prospective lower tier participant shall provide immediate written notice to the person to which this proposal is submitted if at any time the prospective lower tier participant learns that its certification was erroneous when submitted or has become erroneous by reason of changed circumstances.	If at anytime during your transactions with the federal government, you determine that you have been barred or will be, give immediate notice to the government. See Executive Order #12549 (13DFR Part 145) for the debarment definitions.
17.	The terms "covered transaction," "debarred," "suspended," "ineligible," "lower tier covered transaction," "participant," "person," "primary covered transaction," "principal," "proposal," and "voluntarily excluded," as used in this clause, have the meanings set out in the Definitions and Coverage sections of the rules implementing Executive Order 12549. You may contact the person to which this proposal is submitted for assistance in obtaining a copy of those regulations (13 C.F.R. Part 145).	These terms are clearly defined in the executive order's boilerplate. The bottom line is that you, your business, or any other association you are involved with that did or is doing business with the government either (1) has never defaulted in their agreement, or (2) should not be banned from transacting business with the government now, based on this loan proposal.

5.	The prospective lower tier participant agrees by submitting this proposal that, should the proposed covered transaction be entered into, it shall not knowingly enter into any lower tier covered transaction with a person who is debarred, suspended, declared ineligible, or voluntarily excluded from participation in this covered transaction, unless authorized by the department or agency with which this transaction originated.	You don't want to do business with anyone you know has been debarred.
6.	The prospective lower tier participant further agrees by submitting this proposal that it will include the clause titled "Certification Regarding Debarment, Suspension, Ineligibility and Voluntary Exclusion Lower Tier Covered Transactions," without modification, in all lower tier covered transactions and in all solicitations for lower tier covered transactions.	You agree to include this clause in every lower tier transaction or proposal.
7.	A participant in a covered transaction may rely upon a certification of a prospective participant in a lower tier covered transaction that it is not debarred, suspended, ineligible, or voluntarily excluded from the covered transaction, unless it knows that the certification is erroneous. A participant may decide the method and frequency by which it determines the eligibility of its principals. Each participant may, but is not required to, check the Non-procurement List.	A participant, such as a bank, may rely on this certificate that you have not been debarred from transacting business with the government. The participant can also set up its own methods to determine the eligibility of the lower tier principals.
11.	Nothing contained in the foregoing shall be construed to require establishment of a system of records in order to render in good faith the certification required by this clause. The knowledge and information of a participant is not required to exceed that which is normally possessed by a prudent person in the ordinary course of business dealings.	The participant is not required to set up an eligibility check system.

9.	Except for transactions authorized under paragraph 5 of these instructions, if a participant in a covered transaction knowingly enters into a lower tier covered transaction with a person who is suspended, debarred, ineligible, or voluntarily excluded from participation in this transaction, in addition to other remedies available to the Federal Government, the department or agency with which this transaction originated may pursue available remedies, including suspension and/or debarment.	If you knowingly enter into a lowered transaction with someone not qualified, the federal government will make sure you don't try it again.

Table 5.10—SBA Standard Form 1846 (Statement Regarding Lobbying).

Item	Comment
The undersigned states, to the best of his or her knowledge and belief, that:	Read this information.
(1) If any funds have been paid or will be paid to any person for influencing or attempting to influence an officer or employee of any agency, a Member of Congress, an officer or employee of Congress, or any employee of a Member of Congress in connection with this commitment providing for the United States to insure or guarantee a loan, the undersigned shall complete and submit Standard Form LLL, "Disclosure of Lobbying Activities," in accordance with its instructions.	Read this information and determine if you need to file Standard Form LLL in regard to lobbying. (Standard Form LLL is available from your local SBA Office).
(2) Submission of this statement is a prerequisite for making or entering into this transaction imposed by Section 1352, Title 31, U.S.C. Code. Any person who fails to file the required statement shall be subject to a civil penalty of not less than $10,000 and not more than $100,000 for each failure.	Read this information.
Signature and Date.	Sign your name and enter the date.
Name and Title.	Enter your printed name and title.

Table 5.11—SBA Standard Form 159 (Policy and Regulations Concerning

Representatives and their Fees)

Item	Comment
An applicant for a loan from SBA may obtain the assistance of any attorney, accountant, engineer, appraiser or other representative to aid him in the preparation and presentation of his application to SBA; however, such representation is not mandatory. In the event a loan is approved, the services of an attorney may be necessary to assist in the preparation of closing documents, title abstracts, etc. SBA will allow the payment of reasonable fees or other compensation for services performed by such representatives on behalf of the applicant.	If you find that you need the help of an attorney, accountant, engineer, appraiser or other professional, the SBA allows you to hire these services for a reasonable fee, although assistance from these professionals is not mandatory and is left to your discretion.
There are no "authorized representatives" of SBA, other than our regular salaried employees. Payment of any fee or gratuity to SBA employees is illegal and will subject the parties to such a transaction to prosecution.	Be wary of any professional who suggesting to you that they are authorized SBA representatives. SBA has no authorized representatives. SBA also prohibits any type of payment ("bribe") to SBA employees.
SBA Regulations (Part 103, Sec. 103.13-5(c)) prohibit representatives from charging or proposing to charge any contingent fee for any services performed in connection with an SBA loan unless the amount of such fee bears a necessary and reasonable relationship to the services actually performed; or to charge for any expenses which are not deemed by SBA to have been necessary in connection with the application. The Regulations (Part 120, Sec. 120.104-2) also prohibit the payment of any bonus, brokerage fee or commission in connection with SBA loans.	If you have a professional or consultant working with you in obtaining your SBA loan, payment is subject to SBA regulations. These regulations also prohibit the payment of bonuses, brokerage fees, or commissions.
In line with these Regulations SBA will not approve placement or finder's fees for the use or attempted use of influence in obtaining or trying to obtain an SBA loan, or fees based solely upon a percentage of the approved loan or any part thereof.	Avoid any professional or consultant who suggests to you that they want as payment a cut from any loan amount you receive.

Fees which will be approved will be limited to reasonable sums of services actually rendered in connection with the application or the closing, based upon the time and effort required, the qualifications of the representative and the nature and extent of the services rendered by such representatives. Representatives of loan applicants will be required to execute an agreement as to their compensation for services rendered in connection with said loan.	SBA wants to assure that any representative that you work with charges reasonable fees appropriate for their services.
It is the responsibility of the applicant to set forth in the appropriate section of the application the names of all persons or firms engaged by or on behalf of the applicant. Applicants are required to advise the Regional Office in writing the names and fees of any representatives engaged by the applicant subsequent to the filing of the application. This reporting requirement is approved under OMB Approval Number 2345-0016.	Provide the SBA with the names of professional, consultants or other persons who are engaged on your behalf.
Any loan applicant having any question concerning the payments of fees, or the reasonableness of fees, should communicate with the Field Office where the application is filed.	If you are not sure that you are being charged reasonable fees, contact you SBA Field Office.

Table 5.12—SBA Standard Form 159 (Instructions Policy and Regulations Concerning Representatives and their Fees)

Item	Comment
The undersigned representative (attorney, accountant, engineer, appraiser, etc.) hereby agrees that the undersigned has not and will not, directly or indirectly, charge or receive any payment in connection with the application for or the making of the loan except for services actually performed on behalf of the Applicant. The undersigned further agrees that the amount of payment for such services shall not exceed an amount deemed reasonable by SBA (and, if it is a participation loan, by the participating lending institution), and to refund any amount in excess of that deemed reasonable by SBA (and the participating institution). This agreement shall supersede any other agreement covering payment for such services.	Read this information.
A general description of the services performed, or to be performed, by the undersigned and the compensation paid or to be paid are set forth below. **If the total compensation in any case exceeds $1,000 (or $300 for: (1) regular business loans of $15,000 or less; or (2) all disaster home loans) or if SBA should otherwise require, the services must be itemized on a schedule attached showing each date services were performed, time spent each day, and description of service rendered on each day listed.**	Read this information.
The undersigned Applicant and representative hereby certify that no other fees have been charged or will be charged by the representative in connection with this loan, unless provided for in the loan authorization specifically approved by SBA.	Read this information.

GENERAL DESCRIPTION OF SERVICES
    Paid Previously $_____
    Additional Amount to be Paid $_____
    Total Compensation $_____
	Provide this information.

(Section 13 of the Small Business Act (15 USC 642) requires disclosures concerning fees. Parts 103, 108 and 120 of Title 13 of the Code of Federal Regulations contain provisions covering appearances and compensation of persons representing SBA applicants. Section 103.13-5 authorizes the suspension or revocation of the privilege of any such person to appear before SBA for charging a fee deemed unreasonable by SBA for services actually performed, charging of unreasonable expenses, or violation of this agreement. Whoever commits any fraud, by false or misleading statement or representation, or by conspiracy, shall be subject to the penalty of any applicable Federal or State statute.)	Read this information.
Dated_____, _____ _____ (Representative) ___By_____	Provide this information.
The Applicant hereby certifies to SBA that the above representations description of services and amounts are correct and satisfactory to Applicant.	Read this information.
Dated_____, _____ _____ (Applicant) ___By_____	Provide this information.
The participating lending institution hereby certifies that the above representations of service rendered and amounts charged are reasonable and satisfactory to it.	Read this information.
Dated_____, _____ _____ (Lender) ___By_____	Provide this information.
NOTE: Foregoing certification must be executed, if by a corporation, in corporate name by duly authorized officer and duly attested; if by a partnership, in the firm name, together with signature of a general partner.	Read this information.

Table 6.1—SBA Standard Form 641 (Request for Counseling).

Item	Comments
A. Name of Company.	Enter the full name of the company and/or business and leave blank if you aren't yet in business.
B. Your Name (Last, First, Middle).	Enter your name, or if the business is a partnership or corporation, enter only one name.
C. Social Security No.	Enter the Social Security number of the person requesting counseling.
D. Telephone (H [Home]) (B [Business]). E. Street. F. City. G. State. H. County. I. Zip.	Enter the information indicated and use the residential address of the person requesting counseling.
J. Tax Identification No.	Enter the tax identification number (usually issued by the state or other jurisdiction of business operation) of the person requesting counseling.
K. Type of Business (check one).	Select the one that reflects the primary business.
L. Bus. Ownshp./Gender.	Select one box that's appropriate for your situation (if your business is jointly planned or owned by a man and a woman, select the "male/female" box).
M. Veteran Status.	Select the appropriate box or boxes for the person requesting counseling.
N. • Indicate preferred date and time for appointment. • Date and Time. • Are you currently in business? Yes or No • If yes, how long? • Type of business (use three to five words):	Answer each item as indicated
O. Ethnic Background.	Select the appropriate choices from "column a" (race) and "column b" (ethnicity) for the person requesting counseling.
P. Indicate, briefly the nature of service and/or counseling you're seeking.	Enter a brief narrative answer.

Q.	• It has been explained to me that I may use further services sponsored by the U.S. Small Business Administration: Yes or No • I have attended a small business workshop: Yes or No • Conducted by:	Answer each item as indicated and provide the name of the person who conducted the small business workshop you attended (if you have not first attended a workshop, you may not be eligible for counseling).
R.	How did you learn of these counseling services?	Select the appropriate answer.
S.	SBA Client (to be filled out by counselor).	Skip this question—the counselor will complete this portion.
T.	Area of counseling provided (to be filled out by counselor).	Skip this question—the counselor will complete this portion.
	I request business management counseling from the Small Business Administration. I agree to cooperate should I be selected to participate in surveys designed to evaluate SBA assistance services. I authorize SBA to furnish relevant information to the assigned management counselor(s) although I expect that information to be held in strict confidence by him/her.	Read this information.
	I further understand that any counselor has agreed not to: (1) recommend goods or services from sources in which he/she has an interest and (2) accept fees or commissions developing from this counseling relationship. In consideration of SBA's furnishing management or technical assistance, I waive all claims against SBA personnel, SCORE, SBDC and its host organizations, SBI, and SBA Resource Counselors arising from this assistance.	Read this information.
	Signature and Title of Requester, Date.	Sign, provide your title, and the date.
	For Use of the Small Business Administration.	Skip this portion.
	Resource, District, and Region.	Skip this portion.

Table 6.2—SBA Standard Form 1100 (Guidelines).

General	Comments
Definition: A cash-flow projection is a forecast of cash funds* a business anticipates receiving, on the one hand, and disbursing, on the other hand, throughout the course of a given span of time, and the anticipated cash position at specific times during the period being projected.	Read this information.
*Cash funds, for the purpose of this projection, are defined as cash, checks, or money orders, paid out or received.	Read this information.
Objective: The purpose of preparing a cash-flow projection is to determine deficiencies or excesses in cash from that necessary to operate the business during the time for which the projection is prepared. If deficiencies are revealed in the cash flow, financial plans **must** be altered either to provide more cash by, for example, more equity capital, loans, increased selling prices of products, or to reduce expenditures including inventory, or allow less credit sales until a proper cash-flow balance is obtained. If excesses of cash are revealed, it might indicate excessive borrowing or idle money that could be "put to work." The objective is to **finally** develop a plan which, if followed, will provide a well-managed flow of cash.	Refer to the example presented in Chapter 4 (Understanding Financial Matters). When cash flow is negative, you must revise the information for the period of time to include a cash injection (such as a loan) in an amount that will provide a positive cash flow.
The Form: The cash-flow projection form provides a systematic method of recording estimates of cash receipts and expenditures, which can be compared with actual receipts and expenditures as they become known—hence the two columns, "Estimate" and "Actual." The entries listed on the form will not necessarily apply to every business, and some entries may not be included which would be pertinent to specific businesses. It is suggested, therefore, that the form be adapted to the particular business for which the projection is being made, with appropriate changes in the entries as may be required. Before the cash-flow projection can be completed and pricing structure established, it is necessary to know or to estimate various important factors of the business, for example: What are the direct costs of the product or services **per unit?** What are the monthly or yearly costs of the operation? What is the sales price per unit of the product or service?	Your cash-flow format should be similar to the example shown in Figure 4.3 (Example of a 12-month Cash-flow Projection).

Determine that the pricing structure provides this business with reasonable breakeven goals (including a reasonable net profit) when conservative sales goals are met. What are the available sources of cash, other than income from sales; for example, loans, equity capital, rent, or other sources?	
Procedure: Most of the entries for the form are self-explanatory; however, the following suggestions are offered to simplify the procedure:	Read this information.
(A) Suggest even dollars be used rather than showing cents.	Round your numbers to the nearest dollar (omit cents).
(B) If this is a new business, or an existing business undergoing significant changes or alterations, the cash-flow part of the column marked "Pre-startup Position" should be completed. (Fill in appropriate blanks only). Costs involved here are, for example, rent, telephone, and utilities deposits before the business is actually open. Other items might be equipment purchases, alterations, the owner's cash injection, and cash from loans received before actual operations begin.	Investments made by you into the business prior to opening the doors represents your pre-startup position.
(C) Next fill in the pre-startup position of the essential operating data (non-cash flow information), where applicable.	Read this information.
(D) Complete the form using the suggestions in the partial form below for each entry.	Read this information.
In order to insure that the figures are properly calculated and balanced, they must be checked. Several methods may be used, but the following four checks are suggested as a minimum:	Follow the suggested checks in developing your cash-flow projection.
CHECK #1: Item #1 (Beginning Cash on Hand —1st Month) plus Item #3 (Total Cash Receipts —Total Column) minus Item #6 (Total Cash Paid Out—Total Column) should be equal to Item #7 (Cash Position at End of 12th Month).	Apply this check to your cash-flow projection
CHECK #2: Item A (Sales Volume—Total Column) plus Item B (Accounts Receivable.—Pre-startup Position) minus Item 2(a) (Cash Sales—Total Column) minus Item 2(b) (Accounts Receivable Collection—Total Column) minus Item C (Bad Debt—Total Column) should be equal to Item B (Accounts Receivable at End of 12th Month).	Apply this check to your cash-flow projection

CHECK #3: The horizontal total of Item #6 (Total Cash Paid Out) is equal to the vertical total of all items under Item #5 (5(a) through 5(w)) in the total column at the right of the form.	Apply this check to your cash-flow projection
CHECK #4: The horizontal total of Item #3 (Total Cash Receipts) is equal to the vertical total of all items under #2 (2(a) through 2(c)) in the total column at the right of the form.	Apply this check to your cash-flow projection
ANALYZE the correlation between the cash flow and the projected profit during the period in question. The estimated profit is the **difference** between the estimated change in assets and the estimated change in liabilities before such things as any owner withdrawal, appreciation of assets, change in investments, etc. (The change may be positive or negative). This can be obtained as follows:	This was part of the old SBA Standard Form 1100 and is not relative to your cash-flow format.
The **change in assets** before owner's withdrawal, appreciation of assets, change in investments, etc., can be computed by adding the following:	—
(1) Item #7 (Cash Position—End of Last Month) minus Item #1 (Cash on Hand at the Beginning of the First Month).	—
(2) Item #5 (t) (Capital Purchases—Total Column) minus Item F (depreciation—Total Column).	—
(3) Item B. (Accounts Receivable.—End of 12th Month) minus Item B (Accounts Receivable—Pre-startup Position).	—
(4) Item D. (Inventory on Hand—End of 12th Month) minus Item D (Inventory on Hand—Pre-startup Position).	—
(5) Item #5 (w) (Owner's Withdrawal —Total Column) or dividends, minus such things as an increase in investment.	—
(6) Item #5 (v) (Reserve and/or Escrow—Total Column).	—
The **change in liabilities** (before items noted in "change in assets") can be computed by adding the following:	—
(1) Item 2(c) (Loans—Total Column) minus 5(s) (Loan Principal Payment—Total Column).	—
(2) Item E (Accounts Payable—End of 12th Month) minus E (Accounts Pay—Position).	—

Analysis	Comments
A. The cash position at the end of each month should be adequate to meet the cash requirements for the following month. If too little cash, then additional cash will have to be injected or cash paid out must be reduced. If there is too much cash on hand, the money is not working for your business.	Read this information.
B. The cash-flow projection, the profit and loss projection, the breakeven analysis, and good cost control information are tools which, if used properly, will be useful in making decisions that can increase profits to insure success.	Read this information.
C. The projection becomes more useful when the estimated information can be compared with actual information as it develops. It is important to follow through and complete the actual columns as the information becomes available. Utilize the cash-flow projection to assist in setting new goals and planning operations for more profit.	Read this information.
Please Note: Public reporting burden for this collection of information is estimated to average 1 hour per response, including the time for reviewing instructions, searching existing data sources, gathering and maintaining the data needed, and completing and reviewing the collection of information. Send comments regarding this burden estimate or any other aspect of this collection of information, including suggestions for reducing this burden, to: Chief, Administrative Information Branch, Room 5000, U.S. Small Business Administration, 409 3rd St., S.W., Washington, D. C., 20416; and to the Office of Information and Regulatory Affairs, Office of Management and Budget, Washington, D. C., 20503.	Read this information.

Table 6.3—SBA Standard Form 1100 (Instructions).

No.	Item	Instructions
1.	**CASH ON HAND** (Beginning of Month)	Cash on hand same as (7), Cash Position Previous Month.
2.	**CASH RECEIPTS** (a) Cash Sales	All cash sales. Omit credit sales unless cash is actually received.
	(b) Collections from Credit Account s	Amount to be expected from all credit accounts.
	(c) Loan or Other Cash Injection	Indicate here all cash injections not shown in 2(a) or 2(b) above. See "A" of "Analysis."
3.	**TOTAL CASH RECEIPTS** (2a + 2b + 2c = 3)	Self-explanatory.
No.	**Item**	**Instructions**
4.	**TOTAL CASH AVAILABLE** (Before Cash Out) (1 + 3)	Self-explanatory.
No.	**Item**	**Instructions**
5.	**CASH PAID OUT** (a) Purchases (Merchandise)	Merchandise for resale or for use in product (paid for in current month).
	(b) Gross Wages (Excludes Withdrawals)	Base pay plus overtime (if any).
	(c) Payroll Expenses (Taxes).	Include paid vacations, paid sick leave, health insurance, unemployment insurance, etc. (this might be 10 to 45% of 5(b)).
	(d) Outside Services	This could include outside labor and/or materials for specialized or overflow work, including subcontracting.
	(e) Supplies (Office and Operating)	Items purchased for use in the business (not for resale).
	(f) Repairs and Maintenance	Include periodic large expenditures such as painting or decorating.
	(g) Advertising	This amount should be adequate to maintain sales volume—include *The Yellow Page* advertising cost.
	(h) Car, Delivery, and Travel	If your personal car is used, charge in this column—include parking and other related costs.
	(i) Accounting and Legal	Outside services, including, for example, bookkeeping.
	(j) Rent	Real estate only (See 5(p) for other rentals).
	(k) Telephone	Self-explanatory.
	(l) Utilities	Water, heat, light, and/or power.
	(m) Insurance	Coverages on business property and products (e.g., fire, liability.; also workman's compensation, fidelity. Exclude "executive" life [include in "5w"]).

	(n)	Taxes (Real Estate).	Plus inventory tax—sales tax—excise tax, if applicable.
	(o)	Interest	Remember to add interest on loan as it's injected (See 2(c) above).
	(p)	Other Expenses (Specify Each)	Unexpected expenditures may be included here as a safety factor.
			Equipment expenses during the month should be included here (non-capital equipment)
			When equipment is rented or leased, record payments here.
	(q)	Miscellaneous (Unspecified)	Small expenditures for which separate accounts would not be practical.
	(r)	Subtotal	This subtotal indicates cash out for operating costs.
	(s)	Loan Principal Payment	Include payment on all loans, including vehicle and equipment purchases on time payment.
	(t)	Capital Purchases (Specify)	Non-expensed (depreciable) expenditures such as equipment, building, vehicle purchases, and leasehold improvements.
	(u)	Other Start-up Costs	Expenses incurred prior to first month projection and paid after the "start-up" position.
	(v)	Reserve and/or Escrow (Specify)	Example: insurance, tax, or equipment escrow to reduce impact of large periodic payments.
	(w)	Owner's Withdrawal	Should include payment for such things as owner's income tax, Social Security, health insurance, and "executive" life insurance premiums.
6.	**TOTAL CASH PAID OUT** (Total 5a thru 5w)		Self-explanatory.
7.	**CASH POSITION** (End of Month) (4 minus 6)		Enter this amount in (1) Cash on Hand following month—See "A" of "Analysis."
	ESSENTIAL OPERATING DATA (Non-cash Flow Information)		This is basic information necessary for proper planning and for proper cash-flow projection. In conjunction with this data, the cash flow can be evolved and shown in the above form.

	A.	Sales Volume (Dollars)	This is an important figure and should be estimated carefully, taking into account size of facility and employee output as well as realistic anticipated sales (actual sales performed—not orders received).
	B.	Accounts Receivable (End of Month)	Previous unpaid credit sales plus current month's credit sales, less current month amounts received (deduct "C" below).
	C.	Bad Debt (End of Month)	Bad debts should be subtracted from (B) in the month anticipated.
	D.	Inventory on Hand (End of Month)	Last month's inventory plus current month merchandise received and/or manufactured minus amount current month sold.
	E.	Accounts Payable (End of Month)	Previous month's payable plus current month's payable minus amount paid during month.
	F.	Depreciation	Established by your accountant, and representing the value of your equipment divided by useful life (in months) as allowed by the IRS.

Table 6.4—SBA Standard Form 4506
(Request for Copy or Transcript of Tax Form Instructions)

Section references are to the Internal Revenue Code.

TIP: If you had your tax form filled in by a paid preparer, check first to see if you can get a copy from the preparer. This may save you both time and money.

Purpose of Form.—Use Form 4506 to get a tax return transcript, verification that you did not file a Federal tax return, Form W-2, information, or a copy of a tax form. Allow 6 weeks after you file a tax form before you request a copy of it or a transcript. For W-2 information, wait 13 months after the end of the year in which the wages were earned. For example, wait until Feb. 1999 to request W-2 information for wages earned in 1997.

Do not use this form to request Forms 1099 or tax account information. See this page for details on how to get these items.

Note: Form 4506 must be received by the IRS within 60 calendar days after the date you signed and dated the request.

How Long Will It Take?—You can get a tax return transcript or verification of nonfiling within 7 to 10 workdays after the IRS receives your request. It can take up to 60 calendar days to get a copy of a tax form or W-2 information. To avoid any delay, be sure to furnish all the information asked for on Form 4506.

Forms 1099.—If you need a copy of a Form 1099, contact the payer. If the payer cannot help you, call or visit the IRS to get Form 1099 information.

Tax Account Information.—If you need a statement of your tax account showing any later changes that you or the IRS made to the original return, request tax account information. Tax account information lists certain items from you return, including any later changes.

To request tax account information, write or visit an IRS office or call the IRS at the number listed in your telephone directory.

If you want your tax account information sent to a third party, complete Form 8821, Tax Information Authorization. You may get this form by phone (call 1-800-829-3676) or on the Internet (at http://www.irs.ustreas.gov).

Line I b.—Enter your employer identification number (EIN) only if you are requesting a copy of a business tax form. Otherwise enter the first social security number (SSN) shown on the tax form.

Line 2b.—If requesting a copy or transcript of a joint tax form, enter the second SSN shown on the tax form.

Note: *If you do not complete line 1b and, if applicable, line 2b, there may be a delay in processing your request.*

Line 5.—If you want someone else to receive the tax form or tax return transcript (such as a CPA, an enrolled agent, a scholarship board, or a mortgage lender), enter the name and address of the individual. If we cannot find a record of your tax form, we will notify the third party directly that we cannot fill the request.

Line 7.—Enter the name of the client, student, or applicant if it is different from the name shown on line la. For example, the name on line 1 a may be the parent of a student applying for financial aid. In this case, enter the student's name on line 7 so the scholarship board can associate the tax form or tax return transcript with their file.

Line 8a.—If want a tax return transcript check this box. Also, on line 10 enter the tax form number and on line 11 enter the tax period, for which you want the transcript.

A tax return transcript is available for any returns of the 1040 series (Form 1040., Form 1040A, 1040EZ, etc.). It shows most line items from the original return, including accompanying forms and schedules. In many cases, a transcript will meet the requirement of any lending institution such as a financial institution, the Department of Education, or the Small Business

---

218

Administration. It may also be used to verify that you did not claim any itemized deductions for a residence.

Note: *A tax return transcript does not reflect any changes you or the IRS made to the original return. If you want a statement of your tax account with the changes, see Tax Account Information on page 1.*

Line 8b.—Check this box only if you want proof from the IRS that you did not file a return for the year. Also, on line 11 enter the tax period for which you want verification of nonfiling.

Line 8c.—If you want only Form(s) W-2 information, check this box. Also, on line 10 enter "Forms(s) W-2 only" and on line 11 enter the tax period for which you want the information.

You may receive a copy of your actual Form W-2 or a transcript of the information, depending on how your employer filed the form. However, state withholding information is not shown on a transcript. If you have filed your tax return for the year the wages were earned, you can get a copy of the actual Form W-2 by requesting a complete copy of your return and paying the required fee.

Contact your employer if you have lost your current year's Form W-2 or have not received it by the time you are ready to prepare your tax return.

Note: *If you are requesting information about your spouse's Form W-2 your spouse must sign Form 4506.*

Line 8d.—If you want a certified copy of a tax form for court or administrative proceedings, Kansas, New Mexico, check the box to the right of line 8d. It will take at least 60 days to process your request.

Line 11.—Enter the year(s) of the tax form or tax return transcript you want. For fiscal-year filers or requests for quarterly tax forms, enter the date the period ended; for example, 3/31/96, 6130/96, etc. If you need more than four different tax periods, use additional Forms 4506. Tax forms filed 6 or more years ago may not be available for making copies. However, tax account information is generally still available for these periods.

Line 12c.—Write your SSN or EIN and "Form 4506 Request" on your check or money order. If we cannot fill your request, we will refund your payment.

Signature.—Requests for copies of tax forms or tax return transcripts to be sent to a third party must be signed by the person whose name is shown on line 1 a or by a person authorized to receive the requested information.

Copies of tax forms or tax return transcripts for a jointly filed return may be furnished to either the husband or the wife. Only one signature is required. However, see the line 8c instructions. Sign Form 4506 exactly as your name appeared on the original tax form. If you changed your name, also sign your current name.

For a corporation, the signature of the president of the corporation, or any principal officer and the secretary, or the principal officer and another officer are generally required. For more details on who may obtain tax information on corporations, partnerships, estates, and trusts, see section 6103.

If you are not the taxpayer shown on line 1a, you must attach your authorization to receive a copy of the requested tax form or tax return transcript. You may **attach a copy of the authorization document** if the original has already been filed with the IRS. This will generally be a **power of attorney** (Form 2848), or **other authorization**, such as Form 8821, or evidence of entitlement (for Title 11 Bankruptcy or Receivership Proceedings). If the taxpayer is deceased, you must send Letters Testamentary or other evidence to establish that you are authorized to act for the taxpayers estate.

Where To File.—Mail Form 4506 with the correct total payment attached, if required, to the **Internal Revenue Service Center** for the place where you lived when the requested tax form was filed.

Note: You must use a separate form for each service center from which you are requesting a copy of your tax form or tax return transcript	
If you lived in:	**Use this address:**
New Jersey, New York (New York City and counties of Nassau, Rockland, Suffolk, and Westchester)	1040 Waverly Ave. Photocopy Unit Stop 532 Holtsville, NY 11742
New York (all other counties), Connecticut, Maine, Massachusetts, New Hampshire, Rhode Island, Vermont	310 Lowell St. Photocopy Unit Stop 679 Andover, MA 01810
Florida, Georgia, South Carolina	4800 Buford Hwy Photocopy Unit Stop 91 Doraville, GA 30362
Indiana, Kentucky, Michigan, Ohio, West Virginia	P.O. Box 145500 Photocopy Unit Stop 524 Cincinnati, OH 45250
Kansas, New Mexico, Oklahoma, Texas	3651 South Interregional Hwy. Photocopy Unit Stop 6716 Austin, TX 73301
Alaska, Arizona, California (counties of Alpine, Amador, Bufte, Calaveras, Colusa, Contra Costa, Del Norte, El Dorado, Glenn, Humboldt, Lake, Lassen, Marin, Mendocino, Modoc, Napa, Nevada, Placer, Plumas, Sacramento, San Joaquin Shasta, Sierra, Siskiyou, Solano, Sonoma, Sutter, Tehama, Trinity, Yolo, and Yuba), Colorado, Idaho, Montana, Nebraska, Nevada, North Dakota, Oregon, South Dakota, Utah, Washington, Wyoming	P.O. Box 9941 Photocopy Unit Stop 6734 Ogden, UT 84409
California (all other counties), Hawaii	5045 E. Butler Avenue Photocopy Unit Stop 52180 Fresno, CA 93888
Illinois, Iowa, Minnesota, Missouri, Wisconsin	2306 E. Bannister Road Photocopy Unit Stop 57A Kansas City, MO 64999
Alabama, Arkansas, Louisiana, Mississippi, North Carolina, Tennessee	P.O. Box 30309 Photocopy Unit Stop 46 Memphis, TN 38130
Delaware, District of Columbia, Maryland, Pennsylvania, Virginia, a foreign country, or A.P.O. or F.P.0 address	11601 Roosevelt Blvd. Photocopy Unit DIP 536 Philadelphia, PA 19255

Table 6.5—SBA Standard Form 4506 (Request for Copy or Transcript of Tax Form).

Item	Comment
Note: *Do Not use this form to get **tax account** information. Instead, see instructions below.*	The purpose of this form is for the lender to verify that the borrower filed taxes, and that the information given the lender matches that received by the Internal Revenue Service.
1a Name shown on tax form. If a joint return, enter the name shown first.	Enter the name shown on the tax for. For a joint return, enter the name shown first.
1b First social security number on tax form or employer identification number (See instructions.)	Enter the first Social Security number shown on the tax form. If you are requesting a copy of a business tax form, then enter your employer identification number (if you don't complete line 1b and, if applicable, line 2b, there may be a delay in processing your request).
2a If a joint return, spouse's name shown on tax form.	For a joint return, enter your spouse's name as shown on the tax form.
2b Second social security number on tax form.	Enter the second Social Security number shown on the tax form if you are requesting a copy or transcript of a joint tax form (if you don't complete line 1b and, if applicable, line 2b, there may be a delay in processing your request).
3 Current name, address (including appt., room, or suite no.), city, state, and ZIP code.	Provide the requested information.
4 Address, (including apt., room, or suite no.), city, state, and SIP code shown on the last return filed if different from line 3.	Provide the requested information only if the information differs from that in line 3.
5 If copy of form or a tax return transcript is to be mailed to someone else, enter the third party's name and address.	Provide the requested information only if you want the records sent to a third party, such as your accountant or the lender.
6 If we cannot find a record of your tax form and you want the payment refunded to the third party, check here.	This is not applicable when you are applying for a loan.
7 If name in third party's records differs from line 1a above, enter that name here (see instructions).	Enter the name of the loan applicant if it is different from the name shown on line 1a. (This may not apply to business loan applications. The loan applicant may be a sole proprietor or other entity such as a corporation. The tax filer may be "John Doe," but the loan applicant may be "John Doe, and Comp."
8 Check only one box to show what you want. There is **no charge** for items 8a, b, and c. a Tax return transcript of Form 1040. series filed during the **current calendar** year and the	Select one box to indicate what you want the IRS to send. As a practical matter, you will receive a tax return transcript (box "a") sooner than any other item listed here and this is the recommended choice. Otherwise, you may wait months for a response. For lender purposes,

		3 prior calendar years. (See instructions).	you only need 8(a). Under normal circumstances, the applicant will not pay anything. If a fee is due, the lender pays (see purpose of form, Table 6.4).
	b	Verification of nonfiling.	
	c	Form(s) W-2 information (See instructions)	
	d	Copy of tax form and all attachments (including Form(s) W-2, schedules, or other forms). **The charge is $23 for each period requested. Note**: *If these copies must be certified for court or administrative proceedings, see instructions and check here.*	
9		If this request is to meet a requirement of one of the following, check all boxes that apply. • Small Business Administration • Department of Education • Department of Veterans Affairs • Financial institution	Follow this instruction.
10		**Tax form number** (Form 1040, 1040A, 941, etc.)	Identify the tax forms that you want and be specific.
11		**Tax period(s)** (year or period ended date). If more than four, see instructions.	Enter the year(s) of the tax form or tax return transcript you want. For fiscal-year filers or requests for quarterly tax forms, enter the date that the period ended (for example, 3/31/96 or 6/30/98). If you need more than four different tax periods, use additional copies of Form 4506. Tax forms filed six or more years ago may not be available for making copies. However, tax account information is generally still available for these periods.
12		Complete only if line **8d** is checked. Amount Due: a Cost for each period. b Number of tax periods requested on line 11 c Total cost. Multiply line 12a line 12b ***Full payment must accompany your request. Make check or money order payable to "Internal Revenue Service."***	Determine the amount due to the IRS for the items you have requested in line 8d. Write either your Social Security number or employer identification number and "Form 4506 Request" on your check or money order. If the IRS can't fill your request, they will refund your payment.
Caution: *Before signing, make sure all items are complete and the form is dated.*			Read this information.

I declare that I am either the taxpayer whose name is shown on line 1a or 2a, or a person authorized to obtain the tax information requested. I am aware that based upon this form, the IRS will release the tax information requested to any party shown on line 5. The IRS has no control over what that party does with the information.	Read this information.
Please Sign Here • Signature. See instructions. If other than taxpayer, attach authorization document. Date. • Title (if line 1a above is a corporation, partnership, estate, or trust) • Spouse's signature. Date.	Requests for copies of tax forms or tax return transcripts to be sent to a third party must be signed either by the person whose name is shown on line 1a, or by a person authorized to receive the requested information.
Telephone number of requester	Provide this information.
Best time to call.	Provide this information.

Table 7.1—Sample Table of Contents Using Numbered Tabs.

Numbered Tabs	Description of Material
1	Company History
2	Owner and Manager Profiles
3	Business Operations
4	Marketing
5	Purpose of Loan
5	Amount of Loan and Use of Proceeds
5	Loan Repayment
6	Financial Summary of Company
6	Balance Sheet
6	Profit and Loss Statement
6	SBA Standard Form 413—Personal Financial Statement
7	Cash-flow Projections
8	SBA Standard Form 4—Application for Business Loan
9	SBA Standard Form 912—Statement of Personal History
10	SBA Standard Form 4 Schedule A—Schedule of Collateral Exhibit A
11	SBA Standard Form 1624—Certificate of Debarment
11	SBA Standard Form 1846—Statement Regarding Lobbying
11	SBA Standard Form 159—Compensation Agreement for Services
12	Resume
12	Organization Chart
13	Tax Information
13	SBA Standard Form 4506—Request for Copy or Transcript of Tax Form
14	Legal Information
15	Other Supporting Information

Table 7.2—Paper Color Guide.

Color	Image
White	Sharp
Gray and tan	Serious and business like
Light or pastel	Peaceful
Natural	Wholesome

Table 7.3—Loan Package Original.

Items	Preparation	Recommended Materials for Printing or Reproduction
Table of contents and narratives	Print or photocopy	Your chosen paper
Original forms	Use the originals	—
Supporting documents and attachments	Use the originals or photocopy	Your chosen paper or quality white paper
Front and back covers	Print or photocopy	Your heavy stock

Table 7.4—Loan Package Reproductions.

Items	Preparation	Recommended Materials for Printing or Reproduction
Table of contents and narratives	Print or photocopy	Your chosen paper or quality white paper
Forms	Photocopy	Your chosen paper or quality white paper
Supporting documents and attachments	Photocopy	Your chosen paper or quality white paper
Original front and back covers	Print or photocopy	Your heavy stock

Table 8.1   Typical BIC Video Titles.

Advertising (ADV)	
Promotion: Solving the Puzzle	
Business Needs (BN)	
America in Jeopardy: The Young Employee & Drugs in the Workplace	American Red Cross: The Many Faces of HIV
Innovators Guide to the SBIR Program	Virtual Offices & Alternative Workplaces
Business Plan (BP)	
How to Really Create a Successful Business Plan	The Business Plan: Your Road Map For Success
SCORE—Business Planning Program	
Specific Business (SB)	
Auto Detailing Video	The Art of Gift Baskets
Events Planning Video	Wedding Planning Video
Silk Flower Arranging	
Business Start-up (BSU)	
Business Made Easier: Starting a Business in Colorado	How to Start and Run a Small Company Volumes 1-4
Franchising and the SBA	How to Really Start Your Own Business
H. Ross Perot: A Vision for Success in the 90's	The Changing Face of Small Business: Emerging Entrepreneurs
Seminars for Small Business-4 Part Series	
Computer/Computer Software (CMP)	
Communicate Collaborate Cooperate	More Time: More Money: Getting it all Done
From Zero to Sixty in Thirty Days	The Business of Customers
Marketing Your Small Business	
Customer Service (CS)	
6 Steps to Improving Customer Service Through Quality Take Care	Building Loyalty: One Customer & One Employee at a Time
How to Deliver Superior Customer Service	How to Find New Customers
Harvey MacKay on Customer Service	Moments of Truth
Exporting (EX)	
Basics of Exporting	SBA-Opportunity Export
SBA-Exporting	The Dollars and Sense of Exporting
Finance (F)	
Financing-SBA Prog. 4	Maximize Cash Flow
How to Survive & Profit in Tough Times	SBA Financing
SBA 504-The Money That Makes America Work	SSA: Planning Your Future with Personal Earnings & Benefit s Est Statement
Raising Capital	When You Build…Bond-Surety Bonds-Financial Security, Construction Assurance
Home Base Business (HB)	
Home-based Business: A Winning Blue print	How to Succeed in a Home Business
Management (MGMT)	
Effective Follow-up	Managing People
Growing the Company	Smart Solutions for Managing Your Time
How to Deal with Buying Objections	Strengthening America's Competitiveness

Marketing (MKT)	
Creating a Winner: The Real Secrets of Successful Marketing	Marketing: Winning Customers with a "Workable" Plan
Marketing Your Small Business	Do It Yourself Marketing
Sales (SLS)	
Closing the Deal	Making Effective Sales Calls
Finding Buyers for Your Product	More Sales More Profit
How to Manage Your Sales Strategy	Preparing for Successful Sales Relationships
Tax Info (TX)	
Business Made Easier: Preparing Your Sales Tax Return	Small Business Tax Education Program 1995)
Federal Tax Deposits: Making Process Simpler	SSA: Employer Year End Reporting
Women Business Ownership (WBO	
Risks, Rewards & Secrets of Running your own Company	WNET—Women's Network for Entrepreneurial Training
The Fortune—Guide for Enterprising Women (see book with same title)	Women's Business Center http://www.onlinewbc.org
Women in Business	
Miscellaneous (MISC)	
1993 Young Entrepreneur Seminar	Business Information Center
Gov. Romer—Smart Growth & Development: Regional Visions	Interview with Robert B. Aglar (State SCORE Representative)
Case Studies on Small Businesses (5 Volumes)	Real-World: Lessons For America's Small Business
Championing America's Entrepreneurs	SCORE
Creating Communities that Work—Dept. of Energy	SBA Seminars Prog. 1, 2, & 3 (Planning, Rural Initiative & Trends)
Doing Business with DOT	

LIST OF FIGURES

Figure 2.1—Resume for Mr. James Butler.

	Mr. James Butler 3345 South Uinta Street Denver, Colorado 80229 (303) 289-5906
Objective	My objective is to own and operate a small, self-contained business providing mobile automotive service for fleet vehicles, privately-owned passenger automobiles and pickup trucks, and smaller commercial trucks in the metropolitan area and other locations.
Qualifications and Experience	• Formally trained in automobile mechanics with a long-term, personal interest in automobiles and mechanics. • Managed the Outside Board for the Plumber's International Union. • Served on the Executive Board for the local union for two years as a liaison between union members and general contractors.
Employment History	**Master Plumber** for The Drainage Company, Denver, Colorado. Installed residential and commercial plumbing. Reason for leaving is a reduction in wages, benefits, and retirement and a lack of opportunity for advancement. 1990 to present. **Journeyman** for Yankton Plumbing, Yankton, Ohio. Installed grease traps in the restaurant industry. Reason for leaving was reduction in benefits. 1985 to 1990. **Apprentice** for Yankton Plumbing, Yankton, Ohio. Trained for installation of kitchen plumbing. 1981 to 1982.
Certifications, Training, and Memberships	Certified in Auto Mechanics, Yankton, Ohio. In 1986, achieved journeyman status in commercial plumbing following a four-year apprenticeship between 1982 and 1983. Member of the Plumbers International Union, Local #562 in Yankton, Ohio (1981 to 1990) and Local #22 in Denver, Colorado (1990 to present). From 1993 to present, served on the Executive Board and supervised the Outside Board, coordinating schedules and arranging for personnel to fill shifts on an emergency basis. Certified in Law Enforcement Education and Training (1987).
Education	1979 to 1982 Yankton High School, General Studies including Business Mathematics, Auto Mechanics I (1979 to 1980), Vo-Tech Auto Mechanics II (1980 to 1981), and Graphic Arts (1980 to 1982).

Figure 2.2—Sample Owner and Manager Profile.

Mr. Butler, proposed owner of All-City Mobile Lube, graduated from Yankton High School, Yankton, Ohio, in 1982. Mr. Butler is certified in automobile mechanics. While attending high school, he received training in automobile mechanics through two programs: Auto Mechanics I (1979 to 1980) and Vo-Tech Auto Mechanics II (1980 to 1981). His training and practical skills in automobile mechanics fully qualifies him to operate All-City Mobile Lube.

Since graduating from high school, Mr. Butler has been employed continuously in the commercial plumbing industry and achieved master plumber status. Because of reduced wages, benefits and retirement programs, Mr. Butler has chosen to examine alternative employment opportunities. His experience in automobile mechanics naturally oriented him toward a business such as All-City Mobile Lube.

Mr. Butler has been a member of the Plumber's International Union since 1981. As a member of Local #22 in Denver, Colorado, he has served on the Executive Board and the Outside Board. During his tenure with the Outside Board, Mr. Butler gained extensive experience with the practical aspects of scheduling where he coordinated schedules and arranged for personnel to fill shifts on an emergency basis. His scheduling experience is directly relevant to the successful operation of All-City Mobile Lube where service is provided by scheduled appointment.

Figure 2.3—Description of a Key Employee in a Public Relations Firm.

Art director Mr. Stanley Chen is responsible for establishing creative themes and strategies and assembling and supervising a team to implement each project. He has proven himself with more than 20 years of design and illustration experience in providing clients with effective marketing solutions. Mr. Chen received his graphic communications degree from the University of Colorado in 1973. He specializes in brochures, annual reports, corporate identity development, advertising and promotional design, and illustration projects.

Figure 2.4—Sample Organization Chart Emphasizing Established Lines of Authority.

EL TACORITO MEXICAN RESTAURANT, INC.

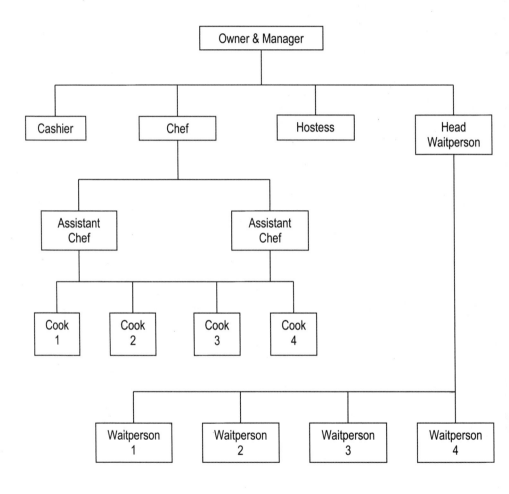

Figure 2.5—Sample Organization Chart Showing a Modified Matrix Management Structure.

DIAMOND PUBLIC RELATIONS, INC.

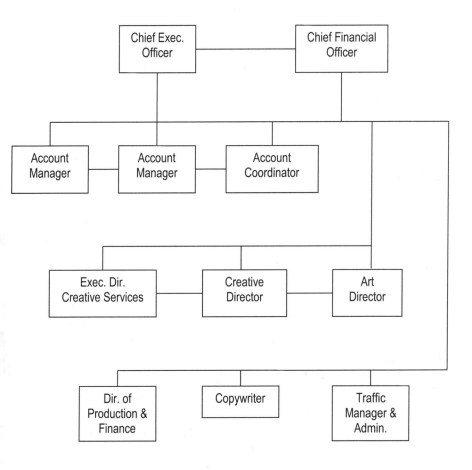

Figure 3.1—Sample Business History for a Home Health-care Business.

Personal Home Health Care
After 20 years of service at General Hospital, retired brain surgeon Dr. Bernice Johnson has identified a need in the community to provide a home health-care service specializing in individuals who have suffered brain trauma resulting in either temporary or permanent brain damage. During the final two years of her service at General Hospital, Dr. Johnson began to develop her business concept, culminating in this proposal. With her training, skills and experience as a brain surgeon, Dr. Johnson is fully qualified to manage cases for individuals with brain injuries. She also has experience in dealing with insurance providers and with Medicare and Medicaid as part of her responsibilities with General Hospital. During the first year of operation, Dr. Johnson (50 percent owner) will serve as Personal Home Health Care's proposed general manager. Mr. Leroy Johnson, a successful business manager with 20 years of experience who will own 30 percent of the business, is proposed as the part-time office manager. Ms. Tiffany Johnson, a registered nurse with two years of experience, is the proposed full-time nursing director and will own 20 percent of the company.

Figure 3.2—Sample Business History for a Restaurant.

Home Cookin' Diner
Ms. Alice Archuleta conceived her idea for establishing the Home Cookin' Diner in 1995 when she observed the long wait experienced by customers with small children at area restaurants during peak dining hours. The following year, as a class assignment in partial fulfillment of an associate's degree in business administration, she developed a business plan for opening a family-style restaurant. As proposed owner and general manager of Home Cookin' Diner, Ms. Archuleta is fully qualified through her 10 years of experience in the restaurant business. During this time, she has been a cashier and waitperson for several area employers, gaining experience in both managing restaurants and meeting customer needs. Her associate's degree in business administration provides her with a sufficient background in business management, assuring a basis for efficient business operation. Ms. Archuleta will hold 60 percent of the proposed company in joint ownership with her husband of six years, Mr. Fernando Gonzales. Mr. Gonzales, a trained and skilled chef with 15 years of experience, will own 40 percent of the business and serve as the head chef and kitchen manager.

Figure 3.3—Sample Business Operations Description for a Service Company.

Business Description
Rocky Mountain Counseling Services, Inc., (RMCS) is a local minority-owned small business servicing clients in the metropolitan area. The company will provide offender-specific programming including Level II education and therapy, relapse prevention, domestic violence, anger management, and cognitive behavioral therapy. RMCS will provide drug and alcohol treatment and monitoring for over 200 clients referred from correction agencies throughout the metropolitan area. Clients accept referral to agencies such as RMCS in lieu of prison sentences. Individual programs are determined by the courts and the clients pay RMCS to provide the services. Ms. Karen Smith, the proposed owner and director of this licensed outpatient treatment program, holds several licenses qualifying her to provide counseling for these types of programs. RMCS initially plans to provide Level I and II education for court-ordered clients, and relapse prevention, intensive outpatient treatment, individual therapy, family counseling, aftercare, and wilderness therapy. The company recognizes the need to add other programs in the future, such as antibuse treatment and monitoring, and urinalysis screening for their drug and alcohol clients to confirm their abstinence. RMCS is licensed by the State of Colorado and by national organizations to provide counseling services for misdemeanants and felons. Certifications held by RMCS are: <ul><li>Colorado Department of Health, Alcohol and Drug Abuse</li><li>National Certified Addictions Counselor II</li><li>Domestic Violence</li></ul> **Note: At this point, you may develop a table or chart showing each proposed office location, services, provided, and status.** One of the most important components of the RMCS day reporting program is client supervision requiring clients to undertake specific activities. For clients under supervisory programs, their progress through levels and subsequent promotion is dependent upon compliance at each of the previous levels. Every client begins at the maximum level of supervision and moves to lesser levels of supervision as the individual masters each higher level. Clients who are non-compliant at the lower levels, may be regressed to more intensive levels. Levels of supervision and client costs vary. RMCS will use a sliding fee scale for clients who have limited resources. **Note: You may insert a table or chart illustrating the various services available and the fees and duration of the treatments.** RMCS will use software products that provide a data management system specifically designed for criminal justice agencies and their service providers. This system is an efficient and cost-effective means of providing accurate reports to the client's referring agency. Client activities are tracked electronically and can be quickly reported. When a referring agency requests a report on a specific client, an up-to-date report is generated within minutes of the original request. Program violations can be identified and reported quickly to the referring agencies. During the intake process, the client receives an identification card that has a bar code.

This card is passed through a reading device, similar to a credit-card reading machine, each time the client enters RMCS's office. The client completes the required activity (e.g., urinalysis, case management meeting) and a code corresponding to that activity is entered into the reading device. These data are stored and downloaded overnight into the computer system of the referring agency. Client progress reports are submitted to the referring agencies on a monthly basis or as requested.

Note: At this point, you may include a table with information on typical day-reporting activities with details on activities, cost to the client, and duration.

Figure 4.1—Example of Amount and Purpose of Loan and Use of Proceeds.

The amount of the requested loan is $45,500 and the purpose of the loan is to assist me in opening an office supply business and retail store. Of the amount requested, $40,000 is to be used as a line of credit to purchase inventory for sale to the general public. The $5,500 balance will be used to finance the purchase of a delivery truck for the business at a cost of $10,500. The line of credit will be secured by the inventory and paid from sales and accounts receivable.

Figure 7.1—Typical Cover Page.

Technical Editing & Writing, Inc.

Loan Proposal in the Amount of $5,000
SBA 7(a) Loan Guaranty Program

For:
Mountain States Bank
Denver, Colorado

Attention:
Mr. John Doe
Senior Vice President

From:
Technical Editing & Writing, Inc.
Ms. Jane Jones, President

Prepared by:
Ms. Jane Jones
Technical Editing & Writing, Inc.
1234 Main Street
Denver, Colorado 80202
Telephone (303) 765-9876
Fax (303) 765-8776

LIST OF REFERENCES

Clean Air Act. Title 42 U.S.C. 7414. Section 114.

Commerce and Trade. Title 15 U.S.C. 645.

Crimes and Criminal Procedure. Title 18 U.S.C. 1001 and 1014.

Debarment and Suspension. Title 13 C.F.R. Part 145. Executive Order 12549.

Debt Collection Act of 1982 and *Deficit Reduction Act of 1984. Title 31 U.S.C.* 3701 *et seq.*

Downes, John, and Jordan Eliot Goodman, 1995. *Dictionary of finance and investment terms.* Hauppauge, NY: Barron's Educational Series, Inc.

Environmental Protection. Title 38 C.F.R. 25161. Executive Order 11738.

Equal Credit Opportunity Act. Title 15 U.S.C. 1691.

Federal Water Pollution Act. Public Law 92-500.

Flood Disaster Protection Act. Title 42 U.S.C. 4011.

Floodplain Management and Wetland Protection. Title 42 C.F.R. 26951 and 26961. Executive Orders.

Freedom of Information Act Office. *Agency Collection of Information,* Form SOP 4004.

Freedom of Information Act. Title 5 U.S.C. 552.

Immigration Reform and Control Act of 1986. Public Law 99-603.

Lead-based Paint Poisoning Prevention Act. Title 42 U.S.C. 4821 *et seq.*

Levinson, Jay Conrad, 1990. *Guerrilla marketing weapons.* New York: Penguin.

Mackay, Harvey, Weekly Column, *The Denver Post,* 21 December 1997, Sunday Edition.

Money and Finance. Title 31 U.S.C. Section 1352.

Occupational Safety and Health Act. Title 15 U.S.C. 651 *et seq.*

Reform and Control Act of 1986. Public Law 9-603.

Right to Financial Privacy Act of 1978. Title 12 U.S.C. 3401.

Robert Morris & Associates, 1997. *Annual statement studies.* Philadelphia: Robert Morris Associates.

Small Business Act. Public Law 85-536.

Standard Operating Procedures. Title 13 C.F.R. Chapter 1, Parts 112, 113, 116, and 117.

U.S. Attorney General. *Title 18 U.S.C.* 100.

U.S. Bureau of the Budget. *Standard Industrial Classification (SIC) Manual.* Washington, D.C.: Government Printing Office, 1994.

U.S. Department of the Treasury, IRS. *U.S. Individual Income Tax Return,* IRS Form 1040. Washington, D.C.: Government Printing Office.

U.S. Small Business Administration. *Application for Business Loan,* SBA Standard Form 4, OMB Approval No.: 3245-0016, Expiration Date: 9-30-97. Washington, D.C.: Government Printing Office, 1993.

U.S. Small Business Administration. *Certification Regarding Debarment, Suspension, Ineligibility and Voluntary Exclusion Lower Tier Covered Transactions*, SBA Standard Form 1624, Expiration Date: 12-92. Washington, D.C.: Government Printing Office, 1992.

U.S. Small Business Administration. *Compensation Agreement for Services in Connection with Application and Loan from (or in Participation with) Small Business Administration*, SBA Standard Form 159, OMB Approval No.: 3245-0201. Washington, D.C.: Government Printing Office, 1991.

U.S. Small Business Administration. *Disclosure of Lobbying Activities*, SBA Standard Form LLL. Washington, D.C.: Government Printing Office.

U.S. Small Business Administration. *Monthly Cash-flow Projection*, SBA Standard Form 1100, OMB Approval No.: 3245-0019, Expiration Date: 9-30-94. Washington, D.C.: Government Printing Office, 1993.

U.S. Small Business Administration. *Personal Financial Statement*, SBA Standard Form 413, OMB Approval No. 3245-0188, Expiration Date: 2-94. Washington, D.C.: Government Printing Office, 1994.

U.S. Small Business Administration. *Request for Copy or Transcript of Tax Form*, SBA Standard Form 4506, OMB Approval No.: 1545-0429. Washington, D.C.: Government Printing Office, 1997.

U.S. Small Business Administration. *Request for Counseling*, SBA Standard Form 641, OMB Approval No.: 3245-0091. Washington, D.C.: Government Printing Office, 1995.

U.S. Small Business Administration. *Schedule of Collateral, Exhibit A*, SBA Standard Form 4 Schedule A, OMB Approval No.: 3245-0016, Expiration Date: 10-31-90. Washington, D.C.: Government Printing Office, 1987.

U.S. Small Business Administration. *Statement of Personal History*, SBA Standard Form 912, OMB Approval No.: 3245-0178, Expiration Date: 7-31-2000. Washington, D.C.: Government Printing Office, 1997.

U.S. Small Business Administration. *Statement Regarding Lobbying—Statement for Loan Guarantees and Loan*, SBA Standard Form 1846. Washington, D.C.: Government Printing Office, 1993.

U.S. Small Business Administration. *The Facts About...Small Business Development Center Program*, FS0043. Washington, D.C.: Government Printing Office, 1996.

Water Act. Title 33 U.S.C. 1318. Section 308.

How to save on attorney fees

How to save on attorney fees

Millions of Americans know they need legal protection, whether it's to get agreements in writing, protect themselves from lawsuits, or document business transactions. But too often these basic but important legal matters are neglected because of something else millions of Americans know: legal services are expensive.

They don't have to be. In response to the demand for affordable legal protection and services, there are now specialized clinics that process simple documents. Paralegals help people prepare legal claims on a freelance basis. People find they can handle their own legal affairs with do-it-yourself legal guides and kits. Indeed, this book is a part of this growing trend.

When are these alternatives to a lawyer appropriate? If you hire an attorney, how can you make sure you're getting good advice for a reasonable fee? Most importantly, do you know how to lower your legal expenses?

When there is no alternative

Make no mistake: serious legal matters require a lawyer. The tips in this book can help you reduce your legal fees, but there is no alternative to good professional legal services in certain circumstances:

- when you are charged with a felony, you are a repeat offender, or jail is possible

- when a substantial amount of money or property is at stake in a lawsuit

- when you are a party in an adversarial divorce or custody case

- when you are an alien facing deportation

- when you are the plaintiff in a personal injury suit that involves large sums of money

- when you're involved in very important transactions

Are you sure you want to take it to court?

Consider the following questions before you pursue legal action:

What are your financial resources?

Money buys experienced attorneys, and experience wins over first-year lawyers and public defenders. Even with a strong case, you may save money by not going to court. Yes, people win millions in court. But for every big winner there are ten plaintiffs who either lose or win so little that litigation wasn't worth their effort.

Do you have the time and energy for a trial?

Courts are overbooked, and by the time your case is heard your initial zeal may have grown cold. If you can, make a reasonable settlement out of court. On personal matters, like a divorce or custody case, consider the emotional toll on all parties. Any legal case will affect you in some way. You will need time away from work. A newsworthy case may bring press coverage. Your loved ones, too, may face publicity. There is usually good reason to settle most cases quickly, quietly, and economically.

How can you settle disputes without litigation?

Consider *mediation*. In mediation, each party pays half the mediator's fee and, together, they attempt to work out a compromise informally. *Binding arbitration* is another alternative. For a small fee, a trained specialist serves as judge, hears both sides, and hands down a ruling that both parties have agreed to accept.

So you need an attorney

Having done your best to avoid litigation, if you still find yourself headed for court, you will need an attorney. To get the right attorney at a reasonable cost, be guided by these four questions:

What type of case is it?

You don't seek a foot doctor for a toothache. Find an attorney experienced in your type of legal problem. If you can get recommendations from clients who have recently won similar cases, do so.

Where will the trial be held?

You want a lawyer familiar with that court system and one who knows the court personnel and the local protocol—which can vary from one locality to another.

Should you hire a large or small firm?

Hiring a senior partner at a large and prestigious law firm sounds reassuring, but chances are the actual work will be handled by associates—at high rates. Small firms may give your case more attention but, with fewer resources, take longer to get the work done.

What can you afford?

Hire an attorney you can afford, of course, but know what a fee quote includes. High fees may reflect a firm's luxurious offices, high-paid staff and unmonitored expenses, while low estimates may mean "unexpected" costs later. Ask for a written estimate of all costs and anticipated expenses.

How to find a good lawyer

Whether you need an attorney quickly or you're simply open to future possibilities, here are seven nontraditional methods for finding your lawyer:

1) **Word of mouth**: Successful lawyers develop reputations. Your friends, business associates and other professionals are potential referral sources. But beware of hiring a friend. Keep the client-attorney relationship strictly business.

2) **Directories**: The Yellow Pages and the Martin-Hubbell Lawyer Directory (in your local library) can help you locate a lawyer with the right education, background and expertise for your case.

3) **Databases**: A paralegal should be able to run a quick computer search of local attorneys for you using the Westlaw or Lexis database.

4) **State bar associations**: Bar associations are listed in phone books. Along with lawyer referrals, your bar association can direct you to low-cost legal clinics or specialists in your area.

5) **Law schools**: Did you know that a legal clinic run by a law school gives law students hands-on experience? This may fit your legal needs. A third-year law student loaded with enthusiasm and a little experience might fill the bill quite inexpensively—or even for free.

6) **Advertisements**: Ads are a lawyer's business card. If a "TV attorney" seems to have a good track record with your kind of case, why not call? Just don't be swayed by the glamour of a high-profile attorney.

7) **Your own ad**: A small ad describing the qualifications and legal expertise you're seeking, placed in a local bar association journal, may get you just the lead you need.

How to hire and work with your attorney

No matter how you hear about an attorney, you must interview him or her in person. Call the office during business hours and ask to speak to the attorney directly. Then explain your case briefly and mention how you obtained the attorney's name. If the attorney sounds interested and knowledgeable, arrange for a visit.

The ten-point visit

1) Note the address. This is a good indication of the rates to expect.

2) Note the condition of the offices. File-laden desks and poorly maintained work space may indicate a poorly run firm.

3) Look for up-to-date computer equipment and an adequate complement of support personnel.

4) Note the appearance of the attorney. How will he or she impress a judge or jury?

5) Is the attorney attentive? Does the attorney take notes, ask questions, follow up on points you've mentioned?

6) Ask what schools he or she has graduated from, and feel free to check credentials with the state bar association.

7) Does the attorney have a good track record with your type of case?

8) Does he or she explain legal terms to you in plain English?

9) Are the firm's costs reasonable?

10) Will the attorney provide references?

Hiring the attorney

Having chosen your attorney, make sure all the terms are agreeable. Send letters to any other attorneys you have interviewed, thanking them for their time and interest in your case and explaining that you have retained another attorney's services.

Request a letter from your new attorney outlining your retainer agreement. The letter should list all fees you will be responsible for as well as the billing arrangement. Did you arrange to pay in installments? This should be noted in your retainer agreement.

Controlling legal costs

Legal fees and expenses can get out of control easily, but the client who is willing to put in the effort can keep legal costs manageable. Work out a budget with your attorney. Create a timeline for your case. Estimate the costs involved in each step.

Legal fees can be straightforward. Some lawyers charge a fixed rate for a specific project. Others charge contingency fees (they collect a percentage of your recovery, usually 35-50 percent if you win and nothing if you lose). But most attorneys prefer to bill by the hour. Expenses can run the gamut, with one hourly charge for taking depositions and another for making copies.

Have your attorney give you a list of charges for services rendered and an itemized monthly bill. The bill should explain the service performed, who performed the work, when the service was provided, how long it took, and how the service benefits your case.

Ample opportunity abounds in legal billing for dishonesty and greed. There is also plenty of opportunity for knowledgeable clients to cut their bills significantly if they know what to look for. Asking the right questions and setting limits on fees is smart and can save you a bundle. Don't be afraid to question legal bills. It's your case and your money!

When the bill arrives

- **Retainer fees**: You should already have a written retainer agreement. Ideally, the retainer fee applies toward case costs, and your agreement puts that in writing. Protect yourself by escrowing the retainer fee until the case has been handled to your satisfaction.

- **Office visit charges**: Track your case and all documents, correspondence, and bills. Diary all dates, deadlines and questions you want to ask your attorney during your next office visit. This keeps expensive office visits focused and productive, with more accomplished in less time. If your attorney charges less for phone consultations than office visits, reserve visits for those tasks that must be done in person.

- **Phone bills**: This is where itemized bills are essential. Who made the call, who was spoken to, what was discussed, when was the call made, and how long did it last? Question any charges that seem unnecessary or excessive (over 60 minutes).

- **Administrative costs**: Your case may involve hundreds, if not thousands, of documents: motions, affidavits, depositions, interrogatories, bills, memoranda, and letters. Are they all necessary? Understand your attorney's case strategy before paying for an endless stream of costly documents.

- **Associate and paralegal fees**: Note in your retainer agreement which staff people will have access to your file. Then you'll have an informed and efficient staff working on your case, and you'll recognize their names on your bill. Of course, your attorney should handle the important part of your case, but less costly paralegals or associates may handle routine matters more economically. Note: Some firms expect their associates to meet a quota of billable hours, although the time spent is not always warranted. Review your bill. Does the time spent make sense for the document in question? Are several staff involved in matters that should be handled by one person? Don't be afraid to ask questions. And withhold payment until you have satisfactory answers.

- **Court stenographer fees**: Depositions and court hearings require costly transcripts and stenographers. This means added expenses. Keep an eye on these costs.

- **Copying charges**: Your retainer fee should limit the number of copies made of your complete file. This is in your legal interest, because multiple files mean multiple chances others may access your confidential information. It is also in your financial interest, because copying costs can be astronomical.

- **Fax costs**: As with the phone and copier, the fax can easily run up costs. Set a limit.

- **Postage charges**: Be aware of how much it costs to send a legal document overnight, or a registered letter. Offer to pick up or deliver expensive items when it makes sense.

- **Filing fees**: Make it clear to your attorney that you want to minimize the number of court filings in your case. Watch your bill and question any filing that seems unnecessary.

- **Document production fee**: Turning over documents to your opponent is mandatory and expensive. If you're faced with reproducing boxes of documents, consider having the job done by a commercial firm rather than your attorney's office.

- **Research and investigations**: Pay only for photographs that can be used in court. Can you hire a photographer at a lower rate than what your attorney charges? Reserve that right in your retainer agreement. Database research can also be extensive and expensive; if your attorney uses Westlaw or Nexis, set limits on the research you will pay for.

- **Expert witnesses**: Question your attorney if you are expected to pay for more than a reasonable number of expert witnesses. Limit the number to what is essential to your case.

- **Technology costs**: Avoid videos, tape recordings, and graphics if you can use old-fashioned diagrams to illustrate your case.

- **Travel expenses**: Travel expenses for those connected to your case can be quite costly unless you set a maximum budget. Check all travel-related items on your bill, and make sure they are appropriate. Always question why the travel is necessary before you agree to pay for it.

- **Appeals costs**: Losing a case often means an appeal, but weigh the costs involved before you make that decision. If money is at stake, do a cost-benefit analysis to see if an appeal is financially justified.

- **Monetary damages**: Your attorney should be able to help you estimate the total damages you will have to pay if you lose a civil case. Always consider settling out of court rather than proceeding to trial when the trial costs will be high.

- **Surprise costs**: Surprise costs are so routine they're predictable. The judge may impose unexpected court orders on one or both sides, or the opposition will file an unexpected motion that increases your legal costs. Budget a few thousand dollars over what you estimate your case will cost. It usually is needed.

- **Padded expenses**: Assume your costs and expenses are legitimate. But some firms do inflate expenses—office supplies, database searches, copying, postage, phone bills—to bolster their bottom line. Request copies of bills your law firm receives from support services. If you are not the only client represented on a bill, determine those charges related to your case.

Keeping it legal without a lawyer

The best way to save legal costs is to avoid legal problems. There are hundreds of ways to decrease your chances of lawsuits and other nasty legal encounters. Most simply involve a little common sense. You can also use your own initiative to find and use the variety of self-help legal aid available to consumers.

11 situations in which you may not need a lawyer

1) **No-fault divorce**: Married couples with no children, minimal property, and no demands for alimony can take advantage of divorce mediation services. A lawyer should review your divorce agreement before you sign it, but you will have saved a fortune in attorney fees. A marital or family counselor may save a seemingly doomed marriage, or help both parties move beyond anger to a calm settlement. Either way, counseling can save you money.

2) **Wills**: Do-it-yourself wills and living trusts are ideal for people with estates of less than $600,000. Even if an attorney reviews your final documents, a will kit allows you to read the documents, ponder your bequests, fill out sample forms, and discuss your wishes with your family at your leisure, without a lawyer's meter running.

3) **Incorporating**: Incorporating a small business can be done by any business owner. Your state government office provides the forms and instructions necessary. A visit to your state office will probably be

necessary to perform a business name check. A fee of $100-$200 is usually charged for processing your Articles of Incorporation. The rest is paperwork: filling out forms correctly; holding regular, official meetings; and maintaining accurate records.

4) **Routine business transactions**: Copyrights, for example, can be applied for by asking the U.S. Copyright Office for the appropriate forms and brochures. The same is true of the U.S. Patent and Trademark Office. If your business does a great deal of document preparation and research, hire a certified paralegal rather than paying an attorney's rates. Consider mediation or binding arbitration rather than going to court for a business dispute. Hire a human resources/benefits administrator to head off disputes concerning discrimination or other employee charges.

5) **Repairing bad credit**: When money matters get out of hand, attorneys and bankruptcy should not be your first solution. Contact a credit counseling organization that will help you work out manageable payment plans so that everyone wins. It can also help you learn to manage your money better. A good company to start with is the Consumer Credit Counseling Service, 1-800-388-2227.

6) **Small Claims Court**: For legal grievances amounting to a few thousand dollars in damages, represent yourself in Small Claims Court. There is a small filing fee, forms to fill out, and several court visits necessary. If you can collect evidence, state your case in a clear and logical presentation, and come across as neat, respectful and sincere, you can succeed in Small Claims Court.

7) **Traffic Court**: Like Small Claims Court, Traffic Court may show more compassion to a defendant appearing without an attorney. If you are ticketed for a minor offense and want to take it to court, you will be asked to plead guilty or not guilty. If you plead guilty, you can ask for leniency in sentencing by presenting mitigating circumstances. Bring any witnesses who can support your story, and remember that presentation (some would call it acting ability) is as important as fact.

8) **Residential zoning petition**: If a homeowner wants to open a home business, build an addition, or make other changes that may affect his or her neighborhood, town approval is required. But you don't need a lawyer to fill out a zoning variance application, turn it in, and present your story at a public hearing. Getting local support before the hearing is the best way to assure a positive vote; contact as many neighbors as possible to reassure them that your plans won't adversely affect them or the neighborhood.

9) **Government benefit applications**: Applying for veterans' or unemployment benefits may be daunting, but the process doesn't require legal help. Apply for either immediately upon becoming eligible. Note: If your former employer contests your application for unemployment benefits and you have to defend yourself at a hearing, you may want to consider hiring an attorney.

10) **Receiving government files**: The Freedom of Information Act gives every American the right to receive copies of government information about him or her. Write a letter to the appropriate state or federal agency, noting the precise information you want. List each document in a separate paragraph. Mention the Freedom of Information Act, and state that you will pay any expenses. Close with your signature and the address the documents should be sent to. An approved request may take six months to arrive. If it is refused on the grounds that the information is classified or violates another's privacy, send a letter of appeal explaining why the released information would not endanger anyone. Enlist the support of your local state or federal representative, if possible, to smooth the approval process.

11) **Citizenship**: Arriving in the United States to work and become a citizen is a process tangled in bureaucratic red tape, but it requires more perseverance than legal assistance. Immigrants can learn how to obtain a "Green Card," under what circumstances they can work, and what the requirements of citizenship are by contacting the Immigration Services or reading a good self-help book.

Save more; it's E-Z

When it comes to saving attorneys' fees, Made E-Z Products is the consumer's best friend. America's largest publisher of self-help legal products offers legally valid forms for virtually every situation. E-Z Legal Kits and the Made E-Z Guides which cover legal topics include all necessary forms and a simple-to-follow manual of instructions or a layman's book. Made E-Z Books are a library of forms and documents for everyday business and personal needs. Made E-Z Software provides those same forms on disk and CD for customized documents at the touch of the keyboard.

You can add to your legal savvy and your ability to protect yourself, your loved ones, your business and your property with a range of self-help legal titles available through Made E-Z Products.

Save On Legal Fees

with software and books from Made E-Z Products™ available at your
nearest bookstore, or call 1-800-822-4566

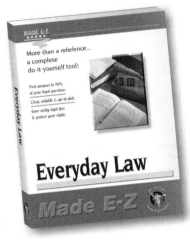

Stock No.: BK411
$24.95 8.5" x 11"
500 pages Soft cover

... Also available as
software—Stock No. SW1185

Everyday Law Made E-Z

The book that saves legal fees every time it's opened.

Here, in *Everyday Law Made E-Z*, are fast answers to 90% of the legal
questions anyone is ever likely to ask, such as:

- How can I control my neighbor's pet?
- Can I change my name?
- What is a common law marriage?
- When should I incorporate my business?
- Is a child responsible for his bills?
- Who owns a husband's gifts to his wife?
- How do I become a naturalized citizen?
- Should I get my divorce in Nevada?
- Can I write my own will?
- Who is responsible when my son drives my car?
- How can my uncle get a Green Card?
- What are the rights of a non-smoker?
- Do I have to let the police search my car?
- What is sexual harassment?
- When is euthanasia legal?
- What repairs must my landlord make?
- What's the difference between fair criticism and slander?
- When can I get my deposit back?
- Can I sue the federal government?
- Am I responsible for a drunken guest's auto accident?
- Is a hotel liable if it does not honor a reservation?
- Does my car fit the lemon law?

Whether for personal or business use, this 500-page information-packed book
helps the layman safeguard his property, avoid disputes, comply with legal
obligations, and enforce his rights. Hundreds of cases illustrate thousands of
points of law, each clearly and completely explained.

MADE E-Z™
PRODUCTS

ss 2001.r3

MADE E·Z® LIBRARY

MADE E-Z GUIDES

Each comprehensive guide contains all the information you need to master one of dozens of topics, plus sample forms (if applicable).

Most guides also include an appendix of valuable resources, a handy glossary, and the valuable 14-page supplement "How to Save on Attorney Fees."

Advertising Your Business Made E-Z G327
Learn the secrets and use the tools of the professionals.

Asset Protection Made E-Z G320
Shelter your property from financial disaster.

Bankruptcy Made E-Z G300
Take the confusion out of filing bankruptcy.

Business Startups Made E-Z G344
Plan and start any home-based or small business.

Buying/Selling a Business Made E-Z G321
Position your business and structure the deal for quick results.

Buying/Selling Your Home Made E-Z G311
Buy or sell your home for the right price—right now.

Collecting Child Support Made E-Z G315
Enforce your rights as a single parent.

Credit Repair Made E-Z G303
All the tools to put you back on track.

Divorce Made E-Z G302
Proceed on your own, without a lawyer.

Employment Law Made E-Z G312
A handy reference for employers and employees.

Financing Your Business Made E-Z G322
Negotiate the best financing and grow your business.

Free Legal Help Made E-Z G339
Enforce your rights—without an expensive lawyer.

Free Stuff For Everyone Made E-Z G347
A complete roadmap to fabulous freebies.

Fund Raising Made E-Z G332
Magnetize big donations with simple ideas.

Get Out of Debt Made E-Z
Learn how to become debt-free.

Incorporation Made E-Z G301
Information you need to incorporate your company.

Last Will & Testament Made E-Z G307
Write a will the right way—the E-Z way.

Limited Liability Companies Made E-Z G316
Learn all about the hottest new business entity.

Living Trust Made E-Z G305
Trust us to help you provide for your loved ones.

Living Will Made E-Z G306
Take steps now to insure Death With Dignity.

Marketing Your Small Business Made E-Z G335
Proven marketing strategies for business success.

Money For College Made E-Z G334
Finance your college education—without the debt!

Multi-level Marketing Made E-Z G338
Turn your own product or service into an MLM empire.

Mutual Fund Investing Made E-Z G343
Build a secure future with fast-growth mutual funds.

Offshore Investing Made E-Z G337
Transfer your wealth offshore for financial privacy.

Owning a No-Cash-Down Business Made E-Z G336
Financial independence without risk, cash, or experience.

Partnerships Made E-Z G318
Avoid double taxation.

Profitable Mail Order Made E-Z G323
Turn virtually any product into a profitable mail order item.

SBA Loans Made E-Z G325
In-depth explanation of required and optional forms.

Selling On The Web Made E-Z G324
Wealth-building, web-building strategies for any size business.

Shoestring Investing Made E-Z G330
Amass more wealth with investments through strategic investing.

Stock Market Investing Made E-Z G331
Pick the best stocks and manage your own portfolio.

Solving Business Problems Made E-Z G326
Identify and solve business problems with proven strategies.

Solving IRS Problems Made E-Z G319
Settle with the IRS for pennies on the dollar.

Successful Resumes Made E-Z G346
Exploit your strengths, gain confidence, and secure that dream.

Winning Business Plans Made E-Z G342
Attract more capital—faster.

By the book...

MADE E-Z™ *books provide all the forms you need to take care of business and save on legal fees – only $24.95 each!*

Everyday Legal Forms & Agreements Made E-Z Stock No. BK407
A do-it-yourself legal library of 301 ready-to-use perforated legal documents for virtually every personal or business need!

Corporate Records Made E-Z Stock No. BK410
Keep your own corporate records current and in compliance... without a lawyer!

Personnel Forms Made E-Z Stock No. BK408
Over 240 documents to manage your employees more efficiently and legally!

Vital Records Made E-Z Stock No. BK412
201 simple and ready-to-use forms to help you keep organized records for your family, your business and yourself!

Collecting Unpaid Bills Made E-Z Stock No. BK409
Essential for anyone who extends credit and needs an efficient way to collect.

Business Forms Made E-Z Stock No. BK414
Instantly organize and track important administrative and planning functions to more efficiently operate your business.

ss 2001.r2

Made E-Z Software	ITEM #	QTY.	PRICE‡	EXTENSION
E-Z Construction Estimator	SS4300		$24.95	
E-Z Contractors' Forms	SS4301		$24.95	
Contractors' Business Builder Software Bundle	SS4002		$49.95	
Corporate Secretary	SS4003		$24.95	
Asset Protection Made E-Z	SS4304		$24.95	
Corporate Records Made E-Z	SS4305		$24.95	
Vital Records Made E-Z	SS4306		$24.95	
Managing Employees	SS4307		$24.95	
Accounting Made E-Z	SS4308		$24.95	
Limited Liability Companies (LLC)	SS4309		$24.95	
Partnerships	SS4310		$24.95	
Solving IRS Problems	SS4311		$24.95	
Winning In Small Claims Court	SS4312		$24.95	
Collecting Unpaid Bills Made E-Z	SS4313		$24.95	
Selling On The Web (E-Commerce)	SS4314		$24.95	
Your Profitable Home Business Made E-Z	SS4315		$24.95	
Get Out Of Debt Made E-Z	SS4317		$24.95	
E-Z Business Lawyer Library	SS4318		$49.95	
E-Z Estate Planner	SS4319		$49.95	
E-Z Personal Lawyer Library	SS4320		$49.95	
Payroll Made E-Z	SS4321		$24.95	
Personal Legal Forms and Agreements	SS4322		$24.95	
Business Legal Forms and Agreements	SS4323		$24.95	
Employee Policies and Manuals	SS4324		$24.95	
Incorporation Made E-Z	SW1176		$24.95	
Last Wills Made E-Z	SW1177		$24.95	
Everyday Law Made E-Z	SW1185		$24.95	
Everyday Legal Forms & Agreements Made E-Z	SW1186		$24.95	
Business Startups Made E-Z	SW1192		$24.95	
Credit Repair Made E-Z	SW2211		$24.95	
Business Forms Made E-Z	SW2223		$24.95	
Buying and Selling A Business Made E-Z	SW2242		$24.95	
Marketing Your Small Business Made E-Z	SW2245		$24.95	
Get Out Of Debt Made E-Z	SW2246		$24.95	
Winning Business Plans Made E-Z	SW2247		$24.95	
Successful Resumes Made E-Z	SW2248		$24.95	
Solving Business Problems Made E-Z	SW2249		$24.95	
Profitable Mail Order Made E-Z	SW2250		$24.95	
Deluxe Business Forms	SW2251		$49.95	
E-Z Small Business Library	SW2252		$49.95	
Sub-total for Software			$	
Made E-Z Guides				
Bankruptcy Made E-Z	G300		$14.95	
Incorporation Made E-Z	G301		$14.95	
Divorce Made E-Z	G302		$14.95	
Credit Repair Made E-Z	G303		$14.95	
Living Trusts Made E-Z	G305		$14.95	
Living Wills Made E-Z	G306		$14.95	
Last Will & Testament Made E-Z	G307		$14.95	
Buying/Selling Your Home Made E-Z	G311		$14.95	
Employment Law Made E-Z	G312		$14.95	
Collecting Child Support Made E-Z	G315		$14.95	
Limited Liability Companies Made E-Z	G316		$14.95	
Partnerships Made E-Z	G318		$14.95	
Solving IRS Problems Made E-Z	G319		$14.95	
Asset Protection Made E-Z	G320		$14.95	
Buying/Selling A Business Made E-Z	G321		$14.95	
Financing Your Business Made E-Z	G322		$14.95	
Profitable Mail Order Made E-Z	G323		$14.95	
Selling On The Web Made E-Z	G324		$14.95	
SBA Loans Made E-Z	G325		$14.95	
Solving Business Problems Made E-Z	G326		$14.95	
Advertising Your Business Made E-Z	G327		$14.95	
Shoestring Investing Made E-Z	G330		$14.95	
Stock Market Investing Made E-Z	G331		$14.95	
Fund Raising Made E-Z	G332		$14.95	
Money For College Made E-Z	G334		$14.95	
Marketing Your Small Business Made E-Z	G335		$14.95	

‡ *Prices are for a single item, and are subject to change without notice.*

continued on next page

	ITEM #	QTY.	PRICE¹	EXTENSION
Owning A No-Cash-Down Business Made E-Z	G336		$14.95	
Offshore Investing Made E-Z	G337		$14.95	
Multi-level Marketing Made E-Z	G338		$14.95	
Get Out Of Debt Made E-Z	G340		$14.95	
Your Profitable Home Business Made E-Z	G341		$14.95	
Winning Business Plans Made E-Z	G342		$14.95	
Mutual Fund Investing Made E-Z	G343		$14.95	
Business Startups Made E-Z	G344		$14.95	
Successful Resumes Made E-Z	G346		$14.95	
Free Stuff For Everyone Made E-Z	G347		$14.95	
Sub-total for Guides			$	
Made E-Z Kits				
Bankruptcy Kit	K300		$24.95	
Incorporation Kit	K301		$24.95	
Divorce Kit	K302		$24.95	
Credit Repair Kit	K303		$24.95	
Living Trust Kit	K305		$24.95	
Living Will Kit	K306		$24.95	
Last Will & Testament Kit	K307		$19.95	
Buying and Selling Your Home Kit	K311		$24.95	
Employment Law Kit	K312		$24.95	
Limited Liability Company Kit	K316		$24.95	
Business Startups Kit	K320		$24.95	
Small Business/Home Business Kit	K321		$24.95	
Sub-total for Kits			$	
Made E-Z Books				
Everyday Legal Forms & Agreements Made E-Z	BK407		$24.95	
Personnel Forms Made E-Z	BK408		$24.95	
Collecting Unpaid Bills Made E-Z	BK409		$24.95	
Corporate Records Made E-Z	BK410		$24.95	
Everyday Law Made E-Z	BK411		$24.95	
Vital Records Made E-Z	BK412		$24.95	
Business Forms Made E-Z	BK414		$24.95	
Sub-total for Books			$	
Labor Law Posters				
☆ Federal Labor Law	LP001		$14.95	
☆ State Specific Labor Law see state listings below			$39.95	

State	Item#	QTY	State	Item#	QTY	State	Item#	QTY
AL	83801		KY	83817		ND	83834	
AK	83802		LA	83818		OH	83835	
AZ	83803		ME	83819		OK	83836	
AR	83804		MD	83820		OR	83837	
CA	83805		MA	83821		PA	83838	
CO	83806		MI	83822		RI	83839	
CT	83807		MN	83823		SC	83840	
DE	83808		MS	83824		S. Dakota not available		
DC	83848		MO	83825		TN	83842	
FL	83809		MT	83826		TX	83843	
GA	83810		NE	83827		UT	83844	
HI	83811		NV	83828		VT	83845	
ID	83812		NH	83829		VA	83846	
IL	83813		NJ	83830		WA	83847	
IN	83814		NM	83831		WV	83849	
IO	83815		NY	83832		WI	83850	
KS	83816		NC	83833		WY	83851	

☆ Required by Federal & State Laws

Sub-total for Posters		$	
TOTAL FOR ALL PRODUCTS		$	
Add Shipping & Handling $3.50 for first item, $1.50 for each additional item		$	
TOTAL PRODUCTS and S & H		$	
Florida Residents add 6% sales tax		$	
TOTAL OF ORDER		$	

¹Prices are for a single item, and are subject to change without notice.

❖ FOR FASTER SERVICE ❖

Order by phone:
(954) 480-8933

Order by fax:
(954) 480-8906

§ 2001 r3

MADE E-Z
PRODUCTS

Name	
Company	
Position	
Address	
City	
State	Zip
Phone ( )	

PAYMENT

❑ check enclosed, payable to:

Made E-Z Products, Inc.
384 S. Military Trail
Deerfield Beach, FL 33442

❑ charge my credit card: ❑ MasterCard ❑ VISA

ACCOUNT NO.   EXP. DATE

Signature: (required for credit card purchases)

Index